SCIENTIFIC ANALYSIS OF GENESIS

An Engineer Examines Genesis

by
Dr. Edward F. Blick

Hearthstone Publishing Ltd.

P.O. Box 815·Oklahoma City, Ok 73101

**A Division Of
Southwest Radio Church Of The Air**

(405) 235-5396   1-800-652-1144   FAX (405) 236-4634

All scripture references are from the King James Version unless otherwise stated.

SCIENTIFIC ANALYSIS OF GENESIS
First Edition, 1991
Copyright © by **Dr. Edward F. Blick**
Oklahoma City, OK

Printed in the United States of America

Published by:
Hearthstone Publishing
P.O. Box 815
Oklahoma City, OK 73101

ISBN 1-879366-12-6

Table Of Contents

Chapter One

Has Science Proved
The Bible Obsolete

Can a man be both a scientist and a Christian? Is there a conflict between science and the Scriptures? Why do some scientists believe in God and yet others reject Him?

Anyone can write a question mark over anything, and some people with a scientific turn of mind seem to take delight in writing a question mark over the Bible and God, shocking and shaking people who have held a faith in God in their hearts. Each of us has built within us a capacity for doubt, and a capacity for faith, with the will of man being the determining factor. Why does one scientist, in possession of the same facts as another, believe and accept Jesus Christ and the teachings of the Bible, and the other reject Him? Since they are both scientists, it couldn't be the facts of science that keep the one from believing. No, it is simply that he exercises his will to doubt rather than to believe. Faith or doubt are determined by the will, not by proof and facts. The believer has *everything to gain and nothing to lose.*

Many educated people today are friendly toward Christianity, but they are not convinced of its truth. They have a sneaking suspicion that it is not intellectually respectable. Many of these people were brought up to accept the Bible and the Christian faith uncritically, but when they began to ask questions for themselves, they found it easier to discard the religion of their childhood than to take the trouble to investigate its credentials. Most of these people do not know that the Christian faith is not founded on wishful thinking or blind acceptance of tradition, but rather on a tremendous body of real objective evidence.

I know that the Bible is the Word of God, and a reader with an open mind should have little difficulty in reaching the same conclusion. God loves you and longs to reveal Himself to you through His Word.

Did you know that for years the Science Research Bureau, headed by the late Dr. Harry Rimmer, publicly offered a reward of one thousand dollars to any person who could prove the existence of a scientific blunder in the Bible? Although that offer was made in twenty-seven different countries, the thousand dollars is still uncollected. In November of 1939 a suit was brought against Dr. Rimmer by a Mr. William Floyd of New York. Mr. Floyd thought that he had found several bona fide scientific blunders in the Bible. The judge, Honorable Benjamin Shalleck of the Fourth District Municipal Court heard both sides of the case and awarded his decision in favor of the Bible (*That Lawsuit Against The Bible*, by Harry Rimmer, W.B. Eerdmans Publishing Co., Grand Rapids, Michigan, 1956). More recently the late Dr. John Grebe, formerly director of both Nuclear and Basic Research at Dow Chemical, Midland, Michigan, has offered a one thousand dollar reward along similar lines.

The absence of error in the Bible is truly remarkable,

for all other ancient books, and even many recent ones, contain scientific blunders and mistakes. In the sacred writings of the Hindus, you find such fantastic nonsense as this: The moon is fifty thousand leagues higher than the sun and shines by its own light; the Earth is flat and triangular and is composed of seven layers — one of honey, another of sugar, a third of butter and still another of wine. This whole seven-layer mass is supposedly borne on the heads of many elephants which, in shaking or stumbling, produce earthquakes. Read the Koran and you find that the stars are torches set in the lower heavens, and that men are made of baked clay.

Why is it that ridiculous teachings like these are not to be found in the Bible, which is much more ancient? Very plainly there is only one explanation — a higher intelligence than that of man presided over the composition of the Bible and preserved its writers from error.

Everything about us points with overwhelming force to a personal Creator whose mind and power are infinite. Dr. George Gallup, director of the Gallup Poll, stated:

> *"I can prove God statistically. Take the human body alone — the chance that all the functions of the individual would just happen is a statistical monstrosity."*

Physicist Dr. Robert Millikan, a Nobel Prize winner, declares:

> *"To me it is unthinkable that a real* atheist *could be a scientist."*

Dr. C.A. Chant, professor of Astrophysics at Toronto University, stated:

"I have no hesitation in saying that at least ninety percent of astronomers have reached the conclusion that the universe is not the result of blind law, but is regulated by a great intelligence."

The Bible says in Psalm 14:1, *"The fool hath said in his heart, There is no God."*

But let us look at some of the sciences and see how they agree with the truth of the Bible. (Two excellent sources for additional material in this area are *Bible-Science Newsletter*, P.O. Box 32457, Minneapolis, Minnesota 55432-0457 and *The Bible And Modern Science*, Henry M. Morris, Colportage Library No. 322, Moody Press, 1968.)

ASTRONOMY

Before the invention of the telescope, scientists regarded the numbers of stars as practically determined. Ptolemy stated that there were one thousand fifty-eight stars. Kepler counted one thousand and five stars and Tycho Brahe catalogued seven hundred seventy-seven. Now these men of science were considered great scientsts in their day — but they were wrong! We now know that there are billions and billions of stars. It is literally impossible to count them. But this is exactly what was written in the Bible thousands of years ago: *"As the host of heaven cannot be numbered . . ."* (Jer. 33:22). So here we see an example out of history where science and the

Bible were in conflict — but as man uncovered more of the truth, he found that true science does not contradict the Bible.

Consider what the Bible has to say about gravity in Job 26:7: *"He . . . hangeth the earth upon nothing."* (No one knows what gravity is or why it is — only its effect.) Consider Isaiah 40:22 where, speaking of God, the prophet Isaiah recorded, *"It is he that sitteth upon the circle of the earth. . . ."* The word "circle" is the Hebrew word *khug* which some Hebrew scholars say may be better translated as "sphericity" or "roundness." The book of Isaiah was written approximately twenty-seven hundred years ago, yet as recently as five hundred years ago, educated men were taught that the Earth was flat.

For more information on the Bible and astronomy, the reader should consult *Science Speaks*, by Peter W. Stoner, Colportage Library No. 346, Moody Press, 1963.

ORNITHOLOGY AND AERODYNAMICS

"But they that wait upon the Lord shall renew their strength; they shall mount up with wings as eagles; they shall run, and not be weary; and they shall walk, and not faint" (Isa. 40:31). In addition to the obvious spiritual truth, this scripture implies a unique quality in the eagle's wings of being able to fly without becoming weary. This is exactly what I discovered in the wind tunnel of the University of Oklahoma while conducting aerodynamic research on birds during the spring of 1971. The eagle has six slotted feathers at the tip of each wing which curve upward in gliding flight. Our wind tunnel measurements indicated these upward-curved slotted-tip feathers reduce

the size of the vortex emanating from each wing tip. This in turn reduces the drag on the wings, thus allowing the eagle to soar large distances in air currents without the need of beating his wings. Thus, twenty-seven hundred years after the scripture in Isaiah was written, science has stumbled onto the same truth.

ARCHAEOLOGY

There exists today not one unquestioned find of archaeology that proves the Bible in error at any point. Jericho has been found with its walls collapsed by Dr. John Garstang, director of the British School of Archaeology in Jerusalem. Dr. Garstang found that the walls had fallen outward even though they were fifteen feet high and ten feet thick — completely substantiating the biblical account. Furthermore, he found from pottery and ceramic evidence that the city had been destroyed about 1400 B.C., coinciding with Joshua's date.

Nebuchadnezzar's furnace, where Shadrach, Meshach, and Abednego were placed, has apparently been found.

Solomon's garrison cities of Hazor, Megiddo, and Gezer (mentioned in 1 Kings) have been found. In addition, his stables, seaport, and copper refineries have been found, and proved that Solomon indeed had a very wealthy empire.

The Hittites are mentioned forty-six times in the Bible. A century ago critics of the Bible claimed that no such people existed. Since that time archaeologists have found Hittite inscriptions revealing that they were one of the powerful nations of ancient times.

The critics also questioned the exodus and conquest of Canaan by the Israelites in 1400 B.C. (a date calculated from the Bible). However, the critics were silenced on this matter when three hundred seventy-seven clay tablets were found in Egypt which described these events. These tablets belonged to Pharaohs Amenhotep III and IV who ruled in the period of 1500-1400 B.C.

Two excellent books which would be helpful to the reader in this area are *An Introduction To Bible Archaeology*, Colportage Library No. 316, and *Genesis And Archaeology*, Colportage Library No. 499, both by Howard F. Vos and published by Moody Press, Chicago in 1959 and 1963 respectively.

METEOROLOGY

The "water cycle" whereby rain water is drained off by rivers into the ocean, then raised back to the sky by evaporation and then carried by wind currents back to the land again, became an accepted fact in this new science about a century ago. Yet this fact was strikingly set forth in the Bible thousands of years ago in Ecclesiastes 1:6-7, *"The wind goeth toward the south, and turneth about unto the north; it whirleth about continually, and the wind returneth again according to his circuits. All the rivers run into the sea; yet the sea is not full; unto the place from whence the rivers come, thither they return again."*

ICHTHYOLOGY

The story of Jonah and the monster of the sea has been difficult for many to believe. It was thought at one time that no fish or whale was large enough to swallow a man. However, the ichthyologists now tell us there are several fish large enough to swallow a man, and three of these are the sperm whale, the white shark, and the rhinodon shark. There have been a number of accounts, some of them well authenticated, of men in modern times having been swallowed by one of the three previously mentioned sea monsters, and then later being rescued alive. For example, an article which appeared in the *Literary Digest* shortly before 1900 presented the account of a Mr. James Bartley who was a seaman on the whaler *Star Of The East*. He was swallowed by a whale in a harpooning foray. A day later when the stomach of the whale was cut open, James Bartley was found alive but unconscious. Following treatment in a London hospital he recovered, but his skin was permanently tanned by the action of the gastric juices.

There is no reason for us not to believe in an actual miraculous intervention by God in the preservation of Jonah's life. The Lord Jesus accepted the story of Jonah as authentic history, and even used it as a symbol of His own coming death and resurrection (Matt. 12:40).

MEDICINE

There are many examples of perfect correlation between the Bible and modern medical science. Consider the following examples which leave little doubt that God is the author of our Bible (taken from *None Of These Diseases*, by S.I. McMillen, M.D., Spire Books, Westwood, New York).

In Genesis 17:12 God is speaking to Abraham: *"And*

he that is eight days old shall be circumcised among you, every man child in your generations. . . ."

Medical doctors have found during the past sixty years that circumcision is a valuable health practice, since it greatly reduces the occurrence of penile cancer in males and cancer of the cervix in their wives. Thus, after many laborious years of experimentation, medical science has at last confirmed, four thousand years later, that the best method of preventing two deadly cancers is circumcision.

Another important item that medical science has recently discovered is the clotting factor in the blood. The textbook *Holt's Pediatrics* reports that a newborn infant has

". . . peculiar susceptibility to bleeding between the second and fifth days of life. Hemorrhages at that time, though often inconsequential, are sometimes extensive; they may produce serious damage to internal organs, especially to the brain, and cause death from shock and exsanguination."

It is felt that this tendency to hemorrhage is due to the absence of the important blood-clotting element, vitamin K. Vitamin K is not manufactured in the baby's intestinal tract until the fifth to the seventh day. Therefore, the first day that one knows for sure that it is safe to perform circumcision is the eighth day, the very day that God commanded Abraham to do so!

Furthermore, there is a second element that promotes the clotting of blood. This element is prothrombin. A chart in *Holt's Pediatrics* shows that when a baby is born, the amount of prothrombin in his bloodstream is less than normal. The curve of prothrombin concentration dips to a very low value on the third day of the baby's life and then skyrockets to a level ten percent above normal on his eighth day. It then levels off to normal values after the eighth day.

Thus, one observes from the concentration of vitamin K and prothrombin that the perfect day to perform a circumcision is the eighth day — a fact known to many doctors and pointed out in the February 1947 *Journal Of The American Medical Association.* So again, we see science correlating with the Bible — but four thousand years later! (Another excellent book on the Bible and medicine is *The Bible And Modern Medicine*, by A. Rendle Short, Moody Pocket Book No. 98, Moody Press, Chicago, Illinois, 1967.)

GEOPHYSICS

Consider the following scripture from the Bible (the paraphrases are the present author's):

> *"And God said, Let there be a firmament* [atmosphere] *in the midst of the waters, and let it divide the waters from the waters. And God made the firmament, and divided the waters which were under the firmament* [lakes, seas, swamps, oceans] *from the waters which were above the firmament* [the water vapor canopy]*: and it was so"* (Gen. 1:6-7).

> *". . . For the Lord God had not caused it to rain*

upon the earth . . . But there went up a mist from the earth and watered the whole face of the ground" (Gen. 2:5-6).

"Where wast thou when I laid the foundations of the earth? . . . When I made the cloud the garment thereof, and thick darkness a swaddling-band [vapor canopy] *for it"* (Job 38:4,9).

The words in the brackets above have been inserted by the author to introduce the notion of a Vapor Canopy Theory or Pre-Flood Greenhouse Theory. This theory states that prior to the flood of Noah the Earth's atmosphere contained a tremendous amount of water vapor, much more than at present[1] [2] [3] [4].

We know that there is enough water in the oceans of the world to cover the entire Earth to a depth of about two miles, if the Earth's topography smoothed out. It is conceivable that some of this water was, before the flood, stored in a great vapor canopy around the Earth. Water vapor in the atmosphere is similar to glass in allowing the short-wave radiation of the sun to pass through, but the long-wave radiation which is re-radiated from the Earth is captured and reflected back to the earth (Fig. 1). Patten[4] believes this water vapor existed in a permanent cloud canopy between five thousand and ten thousand feet altitude.

Hence, this water-vapor blanket would produce a uniformly warm, subtropical climate over the entire surface of the Earth from the North Pole to the South Pole. This uniform climate would have caused meteorological conditions which are much different than those

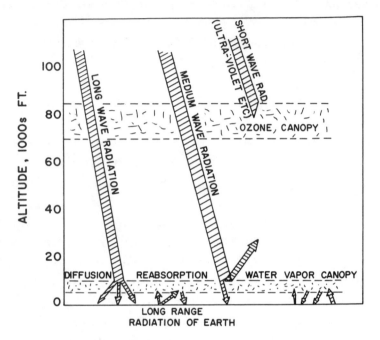

GREENHOUSE MODEL OF PREFLOOD EARTH LIGHT
ABSORPTION, DIFFUSION & REFLECTION

FIGURE 1

which occur today. High winds, storms, etc. would be unknown since they result basically from temperature differences. It is unlikely that rain could have been produced, even though there could have been a continuous interchange of water near the surface by the water condensing as dew at night and evaporating during the day. This inference is supported by the previously quoted scripture in Genesis 2:5-6.

In addition, with no water except gaseous water vapor in the air, the rainbow would be unknown until after the flood, when its first appearance made it a beautiful and striking token of God's promise to Noah (Gen. 9:13-15). The cold ocean waters of today hold ninety percent of the CO_2. The warm ocean waters of the ancient earth could not have held as much CO_2, hence its atmosphere would have been much richer in CO_2.

But, is there any geological evidence that would tend to support this theory? The answer is definitely yes! Coral reefs formed by sea creatures that can live only in warm waters have been found so far north that it is believed now that they underlie the North Pole itself. Tropical animals have been found fossilized not only in Siberia, Greenland, and Alaska, but in practically every region in the world. Fossil ferns and other tropical and temperate vegetation, along with coal beds have been found in the great continent of Antarctica. A warm humid atmosphere rich in CO_2 would produce a great abundance of plant life — just what the fossil record shows.

The Siberian deposits of elephants should also be mentioned (Fig. 2). Literally millions of these animals have been entombed in the frozen soil in much of Siberia. A regular trade in fossil ivory has afforded livelihood to

FIGURE 2

GEOLOGICAL EVIDENCE FOR CANOPY

1. Petrified forests in most deserts of the world
2. Coral reefs near North Pole
3. Coal beds in Antarctica
4. Frozen fruit tree 90 feet high with ripe fruit in frozen Siberia
5. Tropical animals found fossilized in Siberia, Greenland, and Alaska

WORLDWIDE EVIDENCE FOR FLOOD-ICE CATASTROPHE

1. Frozen-drowned mammoths in Siberia
2. Ice dumps 3 miles deep at North Magnetic Pole
3. Ice dumps 5,000 feet thick below sea level in Antarctica
4. Radial ice-flow patterns about magnetic poles
5. Ice and lava interwoven together in eastern Washington
6. Volcanic ash intermixed with ice 5,000 feet below sea level in Antartica

SIBERIAN EVIDENCE FOR FLOOD-ICE CATASTROPHE

1. Untold thousands of mammoths, rhinos, etc. found frozen in Siberia — congested blood indicated drowning death
2. Explorer Baron Edward Toll found intact mammoth near Beresovka, Siberia:
   A. Colagen gelatin in tusks and lips showed no decomposition — sudden freezing required
   B. Digestive tract — 27 pounds of subtropical vegetation, all partly undigested, partly still green
   C. Mouth contained unswallowed and partly masticated grass
   D. Muscle tissue — firm, marbled in fat. Experts noted lack of water — separation in cells indicated sudden temperature below -150 F.
   E. Reproductive system — male mammoth was quick — frozen with erection, indicating sudden death.

the natives of this region since at least 900 A.D. In the more northern parts of the country large numbers of mammoths have been preserved. A number of mammoth carcasses have been found in a standing upright position in the ground as if they had sunk down where they lived and had been frozen in that position. Dramatic evidence of the congested blood in the blood vessels of the frozen mammoths proved that they died by *drowning* in spite of the fact that the modern elephant is a very strong and long swimmer! The remains of the last meal, consisting of elephant grass and other semi-tropical plants now foreign to that region, have been found in their stomachs. Other animals such as rhinoceros, oxen, and sheep have also been found frozen in the Earth of Siberia. The lack of decomposition throughout the mammoth's bodies and the lack of water separation in body cells convinced experts that the mammoths were suddenly frozen at minus 150° F or below.

All of this evidence led British scientist Sir Henry Howorth[5] to conclude that a very great cataclysm and catastrophe occurred in the form of a widespread flood of waters which not only killed the animals and buried them under continuous beds of loam and gravel, but also was accompanied by a great and sudden change in climate which froze the animal flesh under the ground. Geographer Donald Patten[4] builds a strong case for the Greenhouse Effect plus a God-sent astral catastrophism which deposited vast ice masses near the magnetic poles. Patten's arguments indicate that an astral body composed of ice crystals was captured in an elliptical orbit about the Earth which resulted in catastrophic flood tides upon the Earth, turbulence and terrific rain storms which depleted most of the water vapor in our atmosphere (Fig. 3). The vast quantities of ice near our magnetic poles could have resulted from the ice crystals (which possess a positive or negative electric charge) travelling down the magnetic lines of flux to the region of our magnetic North Pole and magnetic South Pole. Patten's calculations show that about six million cubic miles were dumped in each hemisphere. (Note: If evolutionary geology were true, it must explain the origin of three septillion calories of heat transfer, which is the amount needed to reduce twelve million cubic miles of water at 70° F to ice. This is enough heat transfer to reduce many Earth atmospheres to absolute zero or to freeze four hundred cubic feet of ice for every square foot of Earth surface.) *"Out of whose womb came the ice? and the hoary frost of heaven, who hath gendered it? The waters are hid as with a stone, and the face of the deep is frozen"* (Job 38:29-30)!!

Another effect of the Greenhouse Theory could have been a reduction in the amount of short-wave radiation reaching the Earth's surface from the sun. This would be caused by the large amount of water vapor and ozone in the atmosphere. Ozone is concentrated in the upper atmosphere zone and in the pre-flood era it was probably in much greater concentration than in our present atmosphere. This would be due to the reduced vertical turbulence in the uniform atmosphere surrounding the Earth which would reduce the turbulent mixing and cause large concentrations at the upper levels and the water vapor would not only shield the Earth from solar radiation but would also partially shield the outer ozone layer from the Earth's long-wave radiation. The Earth's long-wave radiation causes the ozone (O_3) to recombine

MODEL OF FLOOD - ICE CATASTROPHE

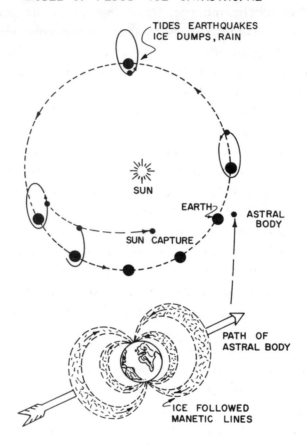

FIGURE 3

back to its normal diatomic state of oxygen (O_2). Thus, the water vapor and ozone would form an effective shield against the sun's short-wave radiation.

One of the most intriguing theories of aging of humans states that short-wave length radiation leads to premature aging and reduces the life span. X-rays, cosmic radiation, and the sun's ultraviolet rays are known to have somatic (non-hereditary) effects as well as genetic effects (gene mutations) which injure the individual but also his descendants as well. Most investigators agree there is no threshold below which ionizing radiation has no effect on living matter.

The pre-flood atmosphere would have far less background radiation than does the present one. Therefore, there must have been fewer somatic and hereditary mutations. Hence, everything, including the climate, favored the continued production of larger, stronger, longer-lived specimens of every type of creature. This, of course, is what we have seen in the fossil record. According to the Bible, many men lived to be more than nine hundred years old before the flood. However, with the vapor canopy precipitated at the time of the flood, the mutation rate speeded up, the size and strength of the average creature deteriorated, many species became extinct, and the length of the lifespan began a steady decline. After the flood, the ages of the patriarchs in the Bible exhibited a slow but steady decline from that of Noah, who lived nine hundred fifty years, through Salah who lived four hundred thirty-three years; Abraham lived one hundred seventy-five years; Moses died an old man at one hundred twenty years; to the familiar biblical seventy-year lifespan (Ps. 90:10). (See Fig. 4 — Note the exponen-

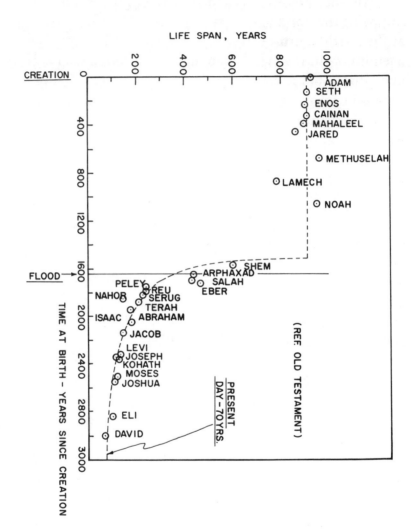

FIGURE 4

tial decay to a step response of first order system.)

Another possible reason for the decline in lifespan following the flood would be the increased level of ozone at the Earth's surface. Jaffe[6] pointed out that ozone is a chemical radical which, when ingested through the lungs and into the blood stream, can be diffused to the cells as a substitute for oxygen. It is known that ozone is capable of producing chromatid breakages in human cell cultures, which are apparently identical to those produced by X-rays. Thus, ozone, even when ingested in only several parts per million, has a toxic effect and will react and injure many types of tissue including reproductive tissue.

It should also be pointed out that the tradition of longevity among the folklore of Egypt, Syria, Persia, India, and Greece is well known. If ancient people (prior to the flood) did live for hundreds of years, then one would certainly expect to find stories and legends concerning their great age to exist in folklore — and this is exactly what we find!

MATHEMATICS AND PROPHECY

There are three hundred prophecies in the Old Testament that were fulfilled by the first coming of Jesus Christ. Professor Peter Stoner, a mathematician in one of California's colleges, gave a homework assignment concerning Old Testament prophecies and probability to students taking his course in mathematical probability. There were forty-eight students in this class and each student was assigned the problem of estimating the probability that Jesus Christ just happened to fulfill one of the prophecies by chance. For example, one student may have been assigned the prophecy in Micah 5:2 which states that the Messiah would be born in Bethlehem. Well, Jesus Christ was born in Bethlehem, so this student had to estimate that out of all the places on the Earth, what were the odds that Jesus Christ would be born in Bethlehem.

To get the total probability that Jesus Christ just by chance happened to fulfill forty-eight prophecies simultaneously, the individual probabilities had to be multiplied together. After doing so, Professor Stoner found that the total probability was one chance out of 10^{180} (one followed by 180 zeros). To put it another way, the chances that Jesus Christ actually is the Son of God are greater than 10^{180} to one. This was calculated using only forty-eight of the three hundred prophecies, so undoubtedly the odds are extremely larger than 10^{180} to one.

The odds of 10^{180} to one are more of a "sure thing" than anything you can predict in your future. For example, let's suppose you are twenty years old and from insurance mortality tables we know the yearly death rate of persons twenty years of age. It turns out that the chances of you dying in the next second are one chance out of 10 billion, or to turn it around, the chances of you living in the next second are 10^{10} to one. 10^{10} is an extremely large number, but infinitesimally small compared to 10^{180}!! To put it another way, the chances that Jesus Christ is actually the Son of God are almost infinitely greater than the chances you have of being alive this next second!!

Chapter Two

Radioactivity And
A Young Earth

We typically hear numbers from evolutionists that the Earth is five or six billion years old, and perhaps that the universe is thirty billion years old. These numbers in the billions are kicked around quite often in reference to the age of the Earth and universe.

However, most dating techniques show that the Earth and solar systems are young — usually less than ten thousand years old. Listed below are just a few evidences.

Atomic clocks, which have for the last half century measured the Earth's spin rate to the nearest billionth of a second, have consistently found that the Earth is slowing down at the rate of almost one second a year. If the Earth were billions of years old, its initial spin rate would have been fantastically rapid — so rapid that major distortions in the shape of the earth would have occurred. So the atomic clocks seem to indicate that the Earth is young.

Direct measurements of the Earth's magnetic field over the past century and a half show a steady and rapid decline in its strength. This decay pattern is consistent with the theoretical view that there is an electrical current inside the Earth which produces the magnetic field. If this view is correct, then twenty-five thousand years ago the electrical current would have been so vast that the Earth's structure could not have survived the heat produced. This would imply that the Earth could not be older than twenty-five thousand years.

Over twenty-seven billion tons of sediment, primarily from our rivers, are entering the oceans each year. Obviously, this rate of sediment transport has not been constant and has probably been decreasing as the looser top soil has been removed. But even if it has been constant, the sediments which are now on the ocean floor would have accumulated in only thirty million years. Therefore, the continents and oceans would not appear to be one billion years old.

The atmosphere has less than forty thousand years worth of helium, based on just the production of helium from the decay of uranium and thorium. There is no known means by which large amounts of helium can escape from the atmosphere. The atmosphere appears to be young.

The rate at which elements such as copper, gold, tin, lead, silicon, mercury, uranium, and nickel are entering the oceans is very rapid when compared with the small quantities of these elements already in the oceans. Therefore, the oceans must be very much younger than a million years.

Evolutionists believe that the continents have existed for at least one billion years. However, the continents are being eroded at a rate that would level them in a relatively short fourteen million years.

The occurrence of abnormally high gas and oil pressures within relatively permeable rock implies that perhaps these fluids were formed or encased less than ten thousand years ago. If these hydrocarbons had been trapped over ten thousand years ago, there would have been leakage which would have dropped the pressure to a level far below what it is today.

There have been no authenticated reports of the discovery of meteorites in sedimentary material. If the sediments, which have an average depth of one and a half miles, were laid down over hundreds of millions of years, many of these steadily falling meteorites should have been discovered. Therefore, the sediments appear to have been deposited rapidly; furthermore, since there have been no reports of meteorites beneath the sediments, they appear to have been deposited recently.

The rate at which meteoritic dust is accumulating on the Earth is such that after five billion years, the equivalent of one hundred eighty-two feet of this dust should have accumulated. Because this dust is high in nickel, there should be an exceedingly large amount of nickel in the crustal rocks of the Earth. No such concentration has been found — on land or in the oceans. Consequently, the Earth appears to be young.

If the moon were billions of years old, it should have accumulated extensive layers of space dust — possibly a mile in thickness. Before instruments were placed on the moon, NASA was very concerned that our astronauts would sink into a sea of dust. This did not happen; there is very little space dust on the moon. Conclusion: the moon is young.

The sun acts as a giant vacuum cleaner which sweeps up about one hundred thousand tons of micrometeoriods per day. If the solar system were just ten thousand years old, no micrometeoriods should remain since there is no significant source of replenishment. A large disk shaped cloud of these particles is orbiting the sun. Conclusion: the solar system is less than ten thousand years old.

Since 1836, over one hundred different observers at the Royal Greenwich Observatory and the U.S. Naval Observatory have made direct visual measurements which show that the diameter of the sun is shrinking at a rate of about one percent each century or about five feet per hour! Furthermore, records of solar eclipses infer that this rapid shrinkage has been going on for at least the past four hundred years. Several indirect techniques also confirm this gravitational collapse, although these inferred collapse rates are only about one-seventh as much. Using the most conservative data, one must conclude that had the sun existed a million years ago, it would have been so large that it would have heated the Earth so much that life could not have survived. Yet, evolutionists say that a million years ago all the present forms of life were essentially as they are now, having completed their evolution that began a thousand million years ago.

Short period comets "boil off" some of their mass each time they pass the sun. Nothing should remain of these comets after about ten thousand years. There are no known sources for replenishing comets. If comets came into existence at the same time as the solar system, the solar system must be less than ten thousand years old.

Jupiter and Saturn are each radiating more than twice the energy they receive from the sun. Calculations show that it is very unlikely that this energy comes from radioactive decay or gravitational contraction. The only other conceivable explanation is that these planets have not existed long enough to cool off.

Stalactites and stalagmites were thought to have taken millions and millions of years to form. However, recent evidence has shown these estimates to be grossly too large. For example, there are stalactites growing in the basement of the Washington Monument in Washington, D.C. Some of the stalactites were found to be as long as five feet in length in 1968. The monument was built in 1923. So, in a period of forty-five years, these stalactites grew about five feet. From this we know that it does not take millions or billions of years for stalactites and stalagmites to form, as was once thought.

There are over eighty scientific indicators of a young earth. Yet, there is no mention of these in most high school biology books. Instead they state that the Earth is billions of years old.

Many evolutionary scientists use various radioactive dating techniques as proof for the age of millions or billions of years, which they place on the Earth.

The first of these techniques I will discuss is the carbon-14 (C^{14}) method. The C^{14} method was developed by Dr. Willard F. Libby from the University of Chicago in the early fifties. He won a Nobel Prize for developing this technique, which was a very deserved award. The technique uses the remains of animals or plants which exchanged carbon with the atmosphere, either directly, by direct ingestion of air which contains carbon, or by eating of material, plants, or animals which contain carbon. Hence, plants, animals, and even humans have carbon in their systems. A portion of this carbon is radioactive carbon — C^{14} (atomic weight equalling fourteen). Ordinary carbon is called carbon-12, which has an atomic weight of twelve. Out of every billion atoms of C^{12}, there are only seven hundred sixty-five atoms of C^{14}. Carbon-14 is a radioactive atom. If you begin with one hundred C^{14} atoms, fifty-seven hundred years later one-half of those would have decayed to nitrogen-14. Therefore, C^{14} is said to have a half-life of fifty-seven hundred years. If another fifty-seven hundred years would pass, then of those fifty C^{14} atoms, twenty-five would have decayed to nitrogen-14, etc. Basically the technique involves taking a sample of material of a bone, piece of wood, or any organic material (a material that was once alive), examining this material, and counting the number of C^{12} and C^{14} atoms. After finding the ratio of C^{14} to C^{12} through a simple mathematical formula, one can then determine the age of this material. One of the limitations of this technique was that if an artifact was older than fifty thousand years, then there would be supposedly too little C^{14} remaining in the artifact to even interpret its age. One example of this would be if you found a dinosaur bone, which according to evolution lived two hundred million years ago, it would have too little C^{14} left to determine its age.

There are certain assumptions which go into this technique. For example, one assumption is that the ratio of C^{14} to C^{12} that exists in our atmosphere, which at present is seven hundred sixty-five atoms of C^{14} to one billion atoms of C^{12}, always remains constant. This is the assumption which Libby made. However, the U.S. space program in the 1960s found that in the upper portions of the atmosphere where C^{14} is formed, there was much more C^{14} than they thought existed. Libby in the 1950s had some information from high-altitude balloons which indicated there was more C^{14} in the upper atmosphere than at the Earth's surface, but he discarded this information. Apparently, his mind was clogged with the evolutionary concept that the Earth was billions and billions of years old. His thinking was that the C^{14} in the upper atmosphere should be the same as that at the Earth's surface. The rockets and missiles going into the upper atmosphere in the fifties and sixties showed that there was more C^{14} there — where it is formed — than on the Earth's surface.

This discovery caused some scientists to modify Libby's original C^{14} method. I call this new method the "space-age C^{14} method." They changed some of the mathematical formulas, which reduced the ages of most of what had been dated to less than fifty thousand years. So this was bad news for the evolutionists. In fact, men like Professor Robert Whitelaw[7] of Virginia Polytechnic and Dr. Melvin Cook[8][9], president of IREC Chemicals and professor of Metallurgy, University of Utah, have studied this data and think that the Earth is perhaps only six to ten thousand years old.

Professor Whitelaw redated fifteen thousand artifacts based on the space-age method. He concluded that none of these were over seven thousand years old. These original dates were published in *Radiocarbon Journal* and other science magazines. Professor Whitelaw is showing that C^{14} dating would predict the creation as being about six to seven thousand years old. This, of course, correlates with the Bible.

There are some amazing facts which came out of the C^{14} method of dating artifacts. These facts were discovered by Professor Whitelaw during his research about C^{14}.

A statistical analysis by Professor Whitelaw[7] of fifteen thousand radiocarbon datings indicates a worldwide disappearance of man and animals for a long period about five thousand years ago. This appears to be a confirmation of the details of the worldwide Genesis flood survived only by Noah, his family, and a boat load of animals. Figure 5 shows that most land-based marine fossils have C^{14} dates of five to seven thousand years!

As can be seen from figures 5 and 6, none of Professor Whitelaw's fifteen thousand radiocarbon dates are over seven thousand years old — which corresponds closely with the age of the Earth according to calculations of some Bible scholars.

Libby, the originator of the C^{14} method back in the early 1950s, had data from upper atmospheric balloon soundings which indicated C^{14} was being formed in the upper atmosphere faster than it was decaying on Earth, but he chose to ignore the data. However, both Cook and Whitelaw had access to additional rocket-sounding measurements (a spin-off of our space program) which also supported the balloon measurements showing a significantly higher rate of formation of C^{14} in the atmosphere than the decay rate on the Earth.

Nearly all specimens of once-living material were found to be datable within the evolutionist time-frame of fifty thousand years. Very few specimens dated back to sixty thousand years and only three of the original fifteen thousand specimens which Whitelaw studied, were considered to be "infinite." These specimens were megapod eggs taken from a Philippine island cave. However, when the known non-equilibrium conditions are used to replace the assumed equilibrium, all of the radiocarbon ages are

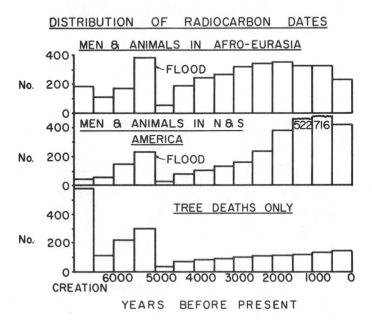

FIGURE 5

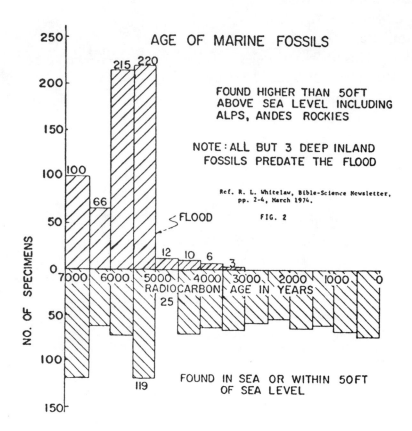

FIGURE 6

telescoped to within less than ten thousand years. This includes published dates on Neanderthal man bones, sabre-tooth tigers, mammoths, coal, natural gas, crude oil, etc.!

This poses a problem for evolutionists. If the geologic column is accurate and, if time extends back to millions (or even billions) of years, for each sample which lends itself to dating there ought to be twenty thousand infinite or undatable samples. While it is true that researchers were looking mainly for items which would date within the fifty thousand-year range (according to their philosophy), *everything* they found was datable within this period of time. This included all samples, even those taken from the maximum depth of any deposit. This supports the position that "things" are not as old as proponents of the geologic column and its attendant long-age dates claim.

Samples in strata identified by investigators as being Pleistocene, Pliocene, and even Eocene (up to fifty million years old, according to evolution) have been laboratory dated as being younger than forty thousand years.

Even coal, petroleum, natural gas, and lignite are dated as being less than fifty thousand years old. According to evolution, these are said to be one hundred million years old.

Most of the oldest dates obtained by the carbon-14 method belong to buried vegetation of all kinds.

More than two hundred twenty of the fifteen thousand dated specimens which Whitelaw studied referred to material considered as fossil material — semi-petrified matter or fossiliferous bed material. Evolutionists often claim this cannot be dated, yet it is being used for dating.

Many dates are of extinct flora and fauna, hitherto thought to be early- and middle-Pleistocene, such as the mastodon, mylodon, sabre-tooth tiger, etc. Almost all are assigned an age of between ten thousand and thirty thousand years.

Many "prehistoric" human remains and artifacts are datable within thirty thousand years, including such famous cases as Neanderthal man, Broken Hill man, Florisbad man, Heidelberg man, the Keilor skull, and Hotu. Furthermore, certain doubt is cast upon the dates of two- to four-million years put by Leakey and others on such forms as the Olduvai Gorge Zinjanthropus and the Omo Valley Australopithecus.

Deep ocean deposits and cores from forty feet below ocean beds, supposed to contain the detritus of the most primitive forms of life, are dated within forty thousand years.

Ancient artifacts from Egypt, Syria, and Iran, dated by archaeologists, indicated radiocarbon dates up to five hundred years younger than has been assumed. This points up the now recognized tendency of ancient historians to exaggerate.

It appears the most ancient dates of human culture are found in the Near East. The oldest "human" dates in the Western Hemisphere clearly are younger than those in the Middle East.

Professor Whitelaw also found these lessons to be learned from carbon-14 (see Figs. 5 and 6).

1. Carbon-14 dates point to a recent creation, particularly when they indicate a recent beginning for cosmic

radiation.

2. Carbon-14 dates can be adjusted to agree with a six to seven thousand age for the universe.

3. Modern man and animals, along with extinct flora and fauna, all appear equally ancient and come with equal suddenness.

4. Carbon-14 dates appear to strengthen the concept that the human race began in the Near East from a few ancestors.

5. Carbon-14 dates seem to indicate a sudden appearance of animals in large numbers all over the world.

6. Carbon-14 dates appear to indicate that trees and low-lying vegetation thrived in areas that today are deserts and polar regions.

7. According to carbon-14 dates, a drastic change took place shortly after creation, a change which adversely affected animals and vegetation. This may indicate the advent of sin into the world.

8. Carbon-14 dates point up a worldwide catastrophe, such as the Noahic flood. This took place about forty-five hundred years ago.

9. Carbon-14 dates seem to indicate a large and widespread human population immediately before the flood.

10. According to carbon-14 dates, there was much vegetation before the flood, vegetation that is now extinct.

11. Carbon-14 dates point up the fact that following a worldwide catastrophe, man, animals, and vegetation started over again.

12. Carbon-14 dates testify that Earth is not billions of years old, nor even millions of years old. The dates

agree with the biblical date of approximately six thousand years as the age for the Earth.

There are some radioactive dating techniques which seem to indicate that the Earth is very old. One of these is the uranium-thorium method. This is a technique used by some scientists to determine the ages of rocks. Uranium-238 (U^{238}) decays to lead-206 (Pb^{206}) plus helium. Its half-life is about four and a half billion years. Using this method, if you find U^{238} and Pb^{206} in a rock, for example, you count the ratio of these atoms in the rock, and make an assumption about the age of the rock, based on a half-life of four and a half billion years. Uranium is leachable by ground water, radon gas can easily move in and out of the system, and some of the intermediate products of uranium and lead include radon gas, radium, and lead-210. Uranium and lead both migrate in shells during geologic times, so as Henry Fall pointed out in *Age Of Rocks*, useful ages cannot be determined with them.

The radiological methods that have been used by some geologists to report ages of rocks up to six billion years are fraught with a great variety of possible experimental errors and shaky assumptions according to Cook[8] [9] and Whitelaw[7]. A great majority of measurements have had to be rejected as useless because of the serious problems inherent in the methods used. For example, in the *Journal Of Geophysical Research*, Vol. 73, No. 14, July 15, 1969, it is reported that lava rocks formed in 1800 and 1801 in Hualalai, Hawaii, show an age of formation of one hundred sixty million to three billion years by the potassium-argon dating method. Yet, the report says with dismay, the age of formation of the rocks is known to be only one hundred seventy years. Another report in *Science*, Vol. 162, page 265, October 11, 1968 shows potassium-argon dates of twelve to twenty-one million years for volcanic rocks known to be less than two hundred years old!

One of the more serious faults with the potassium-argon and other "radioactive clock" techniques is that the original amount of material must be known in order to set the clock to zero.[10] Unfortunately, there were no scientists available to record these initial conditions. If you are an evolutionist and inclined to believe the Earth is billions of years old, then it is convenient for you to assume a large amount of parent element and little or no daughter elements. You now have a technique for generating ages of rocks as millions and billions of years!

Another problem with these radioactive methods is that it is known that many of the daughter elements can easily be leached in and out of the rocks. If this occurs, the method is useless. There is also evidence available now that indicates that the radioactive reactions can be substantially increased by an increase in the flux of neutrinos.[11] The evidence of exploding supernova in nearby stars (with their large fluxes of neutrinos) in the recent past would have sped up radioactive reaction rates on Earth and knocked the whole dating technique into a cocked hat!

An even more important problem for uranium-thorium dating methods is the evidence pointing to free neutron capture by lead, which would change its isotopic value. Thus, lead-206 may be changed to lead-207 and lead-207 to lead-208. According to Dr. Melvin Cook,[9] literally all of the so-called radiogenic isotopes of lead found in uranium-thorium systems may possibly be accounted for by this process alone. Hence, the uranium-thorium rocks in the Earth may all be quite young and not millions or billions of years in age.

Still another problem is that constant radiation produces neutrinos. Neutrinos affect the radioactive decay rate. Any change in the rate or cause of radiation would then change the radioactive decay rate. Phenomena such as change in the Earth's magnetic field or supernova explosions in nearby stars, which are accepted as having occurred in the past, would probably increase the rate of radioactive decay.

These radiological techniques were used on moon rocks, as well. NASA reported that the moon rocks were two to eight billion years old. However, scientists at the Rice University Department of Geology and Space Science said that rare gases found in the rocks, used for age dating, did not come from radiogenic sources, but from a solar wind during a period of one to two thousand years ago. Also, it has been noted that the moon rocks were glazed. In order for moon rocks to have become glazed, they stated that they would have had to been heated to a temperature of 1000° to 1300° centigrade. It is known that potassium vaporizes at 744° centigrade so that if one uses the potassium-argon technique, it would be worthless. Yet, this is the method NASA used to date the moon rocks. Scientists at Rice University and other well known scientists such as Dr. Melvin Cook, Nobel Prize medalist, say that their analysis indicates the moon rocks are perhaps at the oldest, ten thousand years of age.

Numerous indicators seem to point to an age of the

Earth considerably less than five billion years. For example, I refer to the analysis and data of Cook[12] and Faul[13] using helium as chronometer. Helium apparently enters our atmosphere from the solar wind and the radioactive decay of uranium rock. If the Earth were billions of years old we should have much more atmospheric helium than we actually have. The atmospheric helium could have accumulated in about ten thousand years, at the present rate of accumulation.

Due to all of this information from the various scientists and the studies which they have conducted, I believe the carbon-14, uranium-thorium, and potassium-argon methods all point toward a recent creation of life on Earth — rather than evolution over a period of millions or billions of years.

Chapter Three

Evolution, Origin Of Life And Probability

During the first part of this century the proponents of the theory of evolution* (hereafter called evolutionists) waged a battle with those scientists (hereafter called creationists) who held to the biblical creation of life as described in the book of Genesis. By the time of the 1930s it appeared that the evolutionists had won their battle because so few opposing voices were heard. However, about thirty years ago a curious thing developed. There was a rebirth of the challenge to evolution and a rising tide of articles and books appeared which presented new evidence that apparently exposed large cracks in the foundation of the theory of evolution and gave support to the biblical claims of creation (see for example references 14-32).

Much of the credit for this renewed battle between creationist and evolutionist goes to the Creation Research

---

* As far as evolution is concerned, the classic definitionof Sir Julian Huxley is as follows: *"Evolution in the extended sense can be devined as a directional and essentially irreversible process occurring in time, which in its course gives rise to an increase of variety and an increasingly high level of organization in its products. Our present knowledge indeed forces us to the view that the whole of reality* is *evolution — a single process of self-transformation"* (Julian Huxley, "Evolution And Genetics" in *What Is Man?*, Ed. by J.R. Newman, New York, Simon and Schuster, 1955).

Society, which is a group of scientists devoted to researching and publishing in the field of scientific creation. Their arguments have not come from religious grounds but from scientific evidence.

The history of science is the history of births, crises, and deaths. The birth is the birth of a theory which may seem to explain known observations. Then a crisis develops. It does not explain some sets of observations or facts. It then dies and a new theory may rise to take its place. The theory of evolution is in the second phase. It is facing at least four crises which I believe will cause its demise in the not-too-distant future.

The four crises confronting evolution at present are:

1. The Second Law of Thermodynamics
2. Fossil gaps
3. No known mechanism, and
4. Mounting evidence for a young Earth.

Thomas S. Kuhn[33] has examined the history of many of the scientific revolutions that toppled old theories and replaced them with new ones. Kuhn has shown that it was only competition between segments of the scientific community that ever actually resulted in the rejection of one previously accepted theory or in the adoption of another. The rejection of an old theory by a new one was often a stormy battle between supporters of both theories. For men who supported the old theory, the new theory reflected too poorly upon much of the scientific work they had already successfully completed.

James Coppedge[34] has noted that when a fashionable idea has the center of the stage in a society, it tries to drive off opposing viewpoints. For example, Maxwell's equations were as revolutionary as Einstein's, and they were resisted accordingly. X-rays were denounced by Lord Kelvin as an elaborate hoax.[33] Thomas Younger's paper on diffraction and interference aroused a storm of protest, even of derision and abuse. His most vocal assailant, Henry Brougham (later Lord Chancellor of England), wrote:

"We wish to raise our feeble voice against innovations that can have no other effect than to check the progress of science and renew all those wild phantoms of the imagination which Bacon and Newton put to flight from her temple. . . ." [35]

During Pasteur's campaign to disprove the Theory of Spontaneous Generation he was attacked by Pouchet who mockingly argued that if the air really contained seeds of life as Pasteur supposed, the seeds would have to be so numerous that the air would be choked with them and have the density of iron.[37]

WHO BELIEVED EVOLUTION AS FACT?

Many rash and patently false assertions (primarily by writers of high school or college freshmen biology texts) as to the "fact" of evolution have been claimed. For example, B.B. Vance and D.F. Miller[37] wrote in their high school textbook:

"All reputable biologists have agreed that

evolution of life on Earth is an established fact."

J.M. Savage[38] in his introductory college biology text states:

"No serious biologist today doubts the fact of evolution. . . . We do not need a listing of evidences to demonstrate the fact of evolution any more than we need to demonstrate the existence of mountain ranges."

However, when one examines the "proofs" for the "fact of evolution," it appears that writers like Vance, Miller, and Savage are shamelessly bluffing.

Not all scientists, nor all biologists accept the statement that evolution is a proven fact. For example, anyone who thinks that only uninformed cranks reject Darwinism should read Dr. W.R. Thompson's foreword to the new edition of Darwin's *Origin Of The Species*, published in the Darwinian Centennial Year as a part of the Everyman's Library series:

"As we know, there is a great divergence of opinion among biologists, not only about the causes of evolution, but even about the actual process. This divergence exists because the evidence is unsatisfactory and does not permit any certain conclusion. It is therefore right and proper to draw the attention of the non-scientific public to the disagreements about evolution. But some recent remarks of evolutionists show that they think this unreasonable. This situation,

where men rally to the defense of a doctrine they are unable to defend scientifically, much less demonstrate with scientific rigor, attempting to maintain its credit with the public by the suppression of criticism and the elimination of difficulties, is abnormal and undesirable in science."

The tone and tenor of other serious scientists opposing the theory of evolution are aptly illlustrated by the following quotes:

"The probability of life originating from accident is comparable to the probability of the unabridged dictionary resulting from an explosion in a printing shop" (Dr. Edwin Conklin, biologist, Princeton University)

". . . Our time is probably the first in which mythology has penetrated to the molecular level!" (Dr. Erwin Chartaff, Columbia University).

"Protoplasm evolving a universe is a superstition more pitiable than paganism" (President Leavitt, Lehigh University).

"Scientists who go about teaching that evolution is a fact are great con men, and the story they are telling may be the greatest hoax ever. In explaining evolution, we do not have one iota of fact" (Dr. T.N. Tahmisian, physiologist, U.S. Atomic Energy Commission)

"Evolutionism is a fairy tale for grown-ups. This theory has helped nothing in the progress of science. It is useless" (Dr. Louis Bounoure, Director of Research, National Center of Scientific Research in France).

"My attempt to demonstrate evolution by an experiment carried on for more than forty years has failed. . . . It is not even possible to make a caricature of an evolution out of paleobiological facts. The fossil material is now so complete that . . . the lack of transitional series cannot be explained as due to the scarcity of the material. The deficiencies are real, they will never be filled. The idea of an evolution rests on pure belief!" (Herbert Nilssen, Director of Botany Institute, Lund University, in *Synthetische Artbildung*, Vol. I and II, 1925).

In addition, there have been evolutionists with the honesty to admit that theory has not been "proven," and although they may still have "faith" in it, they have pointed out this lack of evidence:

"There are seven basic assumptions not mentioned during discussions of evolution. . . . The first point I should like to make is that the seven assumptions by their nature are not capable of experimental verification. . . . The evidence that supports [the general theory of evolution] *is not sufficiently strong to allow us to consider it as anything more than a working*

hypothesis" (G.A. Kerkut, Professor of Bio-
chemistry, in *Implications Of Evolution*,
Pergamon Press, 1960).

John T. Bonner, eminent biologist, wrote in review
of Kerkut's book:

*"This is a book with a disturbing message; it
points to some unseemly cracks in the foundations. One is disturbed because what it said gives
us the uneasy feeling that we knew it for a long
time deep down but were never willing to admit
this even to ourselves . . . ."(American Scientist,*
Vol. 49, June 1961).

"With the failure of these many efforts [to create
life], *science was left in the embarrassing position
of having to postulate theories of living origins
which it could not demonstrate. . . . Of having
to create a mythology of its own; namely, the
assumption that what could not be proved to
take place today, had, in truth taken place in the
primeval past"* (Loren Eisley, anthropologist, in
Immense Journey, 1957).

The prestigious British science journal, *Nature*, has
recently included a large number of items critical of
evolution. For example, Professor J.W. Fairbairn of the
School of Pharmacy, University of London, wrote:

*"It is now belatedly coming to be realized that
evolutionary speculation has had a deleterious*

effect on practical taxonomy. . . . There is a curious dishonesty about this in much biological writing. . . ." [39]

Another correspondent to *Nature* touches upon the subject of non-believers:

"There are more anti-Darwinists in British universities than you seem to realize. Among them is a friend of mine who holds a chair in a department of pure science 'in a field bearing on the evolution question,' to use your phrase. If his friends ask why he keeps quiet about his unorthodox views, he replies in words like those used recently in another connection by Professor Ian Roxburgh:'. . . There is a powerful establishment and a belief system. There are power seekers and career men, and if someone challenges the establishment he should not expect a sympathetic hearing.' . . . The majority of biologists accept the prevailing view uncritically — just as a great many competent Russian biologists were once brainwashed into accepting Lysenko's quackery. Others have thought for themselves and came to realize the flaws in contemporary Darwinism. But for them to speak out would be to invite ridicule and would probably ruin their careers." [27]

Obviously there is an overwhelming pressure to accept evolution in the life sciences in most universities. When I was the Assistant Dean of the Graduate College, I questioned several graduate students in the life sciences at

the University of Oklahoma. They told me that they did not
believe they could obtain their Ph.D. degree if their graduate committee knew they were non-believers of evolution!
William Randolph Hearst, Jr.[41] once wrote about pressure
from fashionable ideas *"which are advanced with such
force that common sense itself becomes the victim."* A person under such pressure may then act, he said, *"with an
irrationality which is almost beyond belief."*

In spite of the reluctance of many anti-Darwinists to
speak out publicly against Darwinism, there are thousands
who have associated themselves with organizations which
actively attack the theory of evolution. One such group in
England and Canada is the Evolution Protest Movement,
110 Havant Road, Hayling Island, Hants., Polloll,
England. An American group is the Creation Research
Society, 2717 Cranbrook Road, Ann Arbor, Michigan
48104. This latter group has over five hundred voting
members (with graduate degrees in science) and fifteen
hundred non-voting members.

THE SECOND LAW OF THERMODYNAMICS

The study of living organisms is normally the
exclusive domain of life scientists (biologists, etc.), while
the Second Law of Thermodynamics is normally considered in the "camp" of the physical scientists and
engineers. In addition to other "duties," it has been used
by this latter group as the "camp watchdog" to insure that
no process or design heads up the "trail" toward "perpetual
motion machines" and other noble but unattainable
"heights." Historically, the biologists have made little
effort to apply the Second Law of Thermodynamics to

their study of living organisms. In all probability this is due in large measure to their lack of study of thermodynamics in their educational backgrounds. This lack of rigor in thermodynamics shows up in their relating the mass of detailed facts of biology, not by logical thought, but by grand sweeps of the imagination (i.e., evolution). Anthony Standen, in his brilliantly amusing yet informative book *Science Is A Sacred Cow*,[35] managed to deftly puncture the ego of many biologists (and probably incurred their undying wrath) with statements such as:

> "... If you take any course in biology, or read any of the textbooks, you will find extremely little that can be called scientific in any scientific sense. For there is practically nothing there but descriptive facts, and facts alone do not make a science. ... Biology is one vast mass of analogies, very different indeed from the cold logical thinking of the physicist."

So perhaps there are some valid reasons for chiding the biologists for neglecting the study of thermodynamics in relation to living organisms.

The Second Law states there exists a universal principle of change in nature which, in the absence of intelligence supplied by any external source, is downhill, not uphill. It can be defined in various ways, in different context as follows:

A. Classical Thermodynamics: In every process taking place in an isolated system the entropy never decreases. Entropy is a measure of the quantity of energy not capable of conversion into work.

B. Statistical Thermodynamics: *"Each quantity of energy has a characteristic quality called entropy associated with it. The entropy measures the degree of disorder associated with the energy. Energy must always flow in such a direction that the entropy increases."* [42]

C. Information Theory: Shannon[43] defined information as the difference between two entropies. Thus entropy is considered to be a measure of the degree to which information is lost or becomes garbled in the transmission process. All real transmission systems on the average either retain all information (zero change in entropy) or they lose information (increase in entropy), but they do not increase the amount of information (decrease in entropy). Thus any natural isolated process can be regarded in any of several ways:

1. As an energy conversion process in which work is being accomplished

2. As a system undergoing a change in order or structure

3. As an information system which is transmitting or utilizing information.

Entropy is a measure of: in the first case, the unavailability of work; in the second case, the decreased order of the system; in the third case, the loss of information.

All of these explanations describe a downhill trend. Living and non-living systems tend to wear out, rust out, or malfunction. Useful energy is lost, disorder increases, information becomes garbled. The Second Law is a conservative or degenerative process and is considered one of the fundamental laws of nature.

The crisis for the theory of evolution is that it postulates an ordered molecules-to-man process has been going on for millions of years. Staple cell life was supposed to have formed out of inorganic molecules. These simple forms of life then were supposed to have evolved into higher forms (an increase in order). Thus evolution is presumably a "creative" process which increases order, and hence it contrasts sharply with the Second Law of Thermodynamics.

Most books promoting evolution never mention the serious problem of the Second Law. Some evolutionists have merely stated that the Second Law does not apply to living systems. However, the processes of life are complex thermochemical processes and obey the laws of thermodynamics. Biochemist Dr. Harold Blum,[44] an evolutionist himself, has stated:

> *"It is one of this law's consequences that all real processes go irreversible. . . . Any given process in this universe is accompanied by a change in magnitude of a quantity called the entropy. . . . All real processes go with an increase in entropy. The entropy also measures the randomness or lack of orderliness of the system, the greater the randomness the greater the entropy. . . . No matter how carefully we examine the energetics of living systems, we find no evidence of defeat of thermodynamic principles. . . ."*

Some evolutionists have responded to the problem posed by the Second Law by denying its applicability to open systems such as the Earth. They say the steady stream of energy the Earth receives from the sun is more than enough to offset the loss of energy due to entropy. However, even for systems which have local temporary growth such as (a) the growth of a pile of bricks into a building, (b) the growth of a seed into a tree, or (c) the growth of a crystal, there must be a coded plan to sift and sort and direct the energy. In the three previous examples: (a) a blueprint directs the erection of the building; (b) the genetic code of the DNA-RNA complex directs the growth of the seed into a tree; and (c) the chemical code implicit in the periodic table of elements directs the formation of the crystal. But from whence come the codes? Obviously architects or engineers provide the first code. Could mindless particles provide the DNA code and the chemical table of elements?

Other evolutionists (see, for example references 45 and 46) imagine an open system with an excess of reactants which will cause a chemical reaction to proceed drastically to the product side by the well-known LeChatelier principle.

Suppose a reversible action A + B = C is possible but little of C is formed. Suppose also that C is a more complex molecule (higher order) and needed in an evolutionary process. If an excess of A or B is added in the open system, C will be produced. Next it is assumed that the product C can be removed from the reaction site by diffusion. If this is possible, then more C can form from the reaction than would be expected thermodynamically. Dr. Emmett L. Williams, a physicist, has examined these processes and concluded ". . . *the crude natural processes do not act this way. Rather, natural processes follow the*

Second Law. . . ." [47] The burden of proof still rests on those who propose this and other non-equilibrium thermodynamics methods as the means to bring order out of disorder.

ORIGIN OF LIFE

The explanation offered by evolution for the creation of life goes something as follows: Many billions of years ago (perhaps two to six) in the midst of the ocean, within an atmosphere of ammonia, methane, hydrogen, and water vapor, electrical charges came into the atmosphere from outside and a reaction occurred which generated amino acids. By random chance, these amino acids formed into protein, and protein is the basic building block of the cell. Then through random chance these proteins came together in the correct arrangement as mitochondria, golgi bodies, chromosomes, chloroplasts, the vacuols, the endoplasmic reticula, the ribosomes, the centrioles, and all the other parts, all of which within themselves are very complex. Through random chance the parts are hypothesized by have united and ultimately the cell itself is said to have come into being.

There are many aspects of this process that have been shown to be improbable and fallacious. Three of the more important obstacles the evolutionists have never been able to explain are:

1. The Earth's atmosphere probably contained oxygen[48] [49] which would have oxidized the organic chemical compounds[50] [6]
2. If there were no free oxygen in the atmosphere, any life

formed would have been destroyed by the sun's unfiltered ultraviolet radiation, which ruptures chemical bonds in protoplasm. Life exists on Earth today because we are shielded from direct ultraviolet radiation by a high level blanket of ozone.[50]

3. The probability of forming one protein molecule by chance has been calculated by French scientist Lecomte du Nouy as one chance out of ten to the power of 243.[51] Swiss mathematician Charles E. Guye calculated the probability as one chance out of ten to the power of 160.[52] Using digital computers to solve a similar problem, Dr. Murphy Eden of MIT and Dr. Marcel Schutzenberger of the University of Paris both concluded that their digital computers showed that evolution was for all practical purposes, impossible.[21] [22]

The first two obstacles put the evolutionist on the "horns of a dilemma," but the third obstacle is really the impenetrable barrier that reduces evolution from a science to a religion. One must have faith of immense proportions to overcome the overwhelming evidence of mathematical probability opposing evolution.

It is instructive to look briefly at the type of probability analysis that du Nouy[53] and others have employed to compute the probability of life resulting by accident.

A.J. White[32] has computed the probability of formation by chance a small protein, one hundred amino acids long, containing twenty different amino acids in a definite sequence from a "primeval soup" where all the Earth's hydrospheric water molecules have been replaced by these twenty different amino acids. The computation is both interesting and startling! For twenty amino acids to be used to construct a protein one hundred amino acids long in a particular sequence, one can compute the total possible number of configurations as 20^{100} or 10^{130}. The Earth's hydrosphere is about 1.37 times 10^9 cubic kilometers in size containing about 10^{47} molecules. Now make the highly unlikely assumption (but favorable for the chances of formation of the protein) that instead of 10^{47} water molecules, there were 10^{47} of our amino acids instead.

Now suppose that all of the 10^{47} amino acids play "musical chairs" and jump to a new position in a different protein molecule, one hundred amino acids long, once every second. Hence, we produce $10^{47}/10^2 = 10^{45}$ proteins every second. Now a year is 3×10^7 seconds long — say 10^8 to "round it off." Hence every year, $10^{45} + 10^8 = 10^{53}$ proteins are formed.

Now, since the total number of configurations is 10^{130}, our amino acids will have to play "musical chairs" for $10^{130}/10^{53} = 10^{77}$ years before we can be absolutely sure that we have constructed our required protein molecule. But some evolutionists say the Earth is "only" about four to six billion years old (round off to 10^{10} years). Therefore, we can compute the odds against forming the protein molecule as $10^{77}/10^{10} = 10^{67}$ to one. Even if we assumed that the amino acids sped up their "musical chairs" game by a factor from once a second to one hundred million times a second, the odds are still 10^{59} to one against this simple molecule having ever formed at all during the entire estimated "evolutionary life span" of Earth in an environment that has been arbitrarily "weighted" to give the protein every last bit of advantage to be formed by pure chance.

The probability of the living bacterium *Escherichia coli* arising from an equilibrium ensemble of hydrogen, carbon, and nitrogen atoms was investigated by Morowitz.[54] He found that the thermodynamic probability of *Escherichia coli* was the infinitesimally small number 10^{-11}! Morowitz then computed the probability of such a molecule occurring once during the entire history of the Earth. He assumed he had an ensemble of atoms equal to the number of atoms in the universe (approximately 10^{100}) with sampling rates of 10^{16} per second and the process continued for about ten billion years (approximately 10^{18} seconds). Utilizing these estimates, Morowitz found that the probability that the bacterium *Escherichia coli* would occur once during ten billion year was one chance out of one followed by one hundred billion zeros! As Boltzmann (1898) said of a similar number relating to the probability of two gases of a 0.1 liter container unmixing themselves — *"One may recognize that this is practically equivalent to never."*

Morowitz also calculated the probability of one of the smallest living cells, *Mycoplasma hominis H39*, arising spontaneously (at least once in ten billion years) in an equilibrium ensemble and found it to be one chance out of one followed by five billion zeros — also equivalent to never.

Dr. James F. Coppedge, Director of the Center for Probability Research in Biology, Northridge, California, has done a considerable amount of analysis of the probability of forming protein molecules by random chance.[34] Amino acids are the basic building blocks of proteins which are a major class of the complex molecules of all living matter. Amino acids of non-living matter have approximately an-equal amount of left- and right-handed forms. But one of the major mysteries of life is that amino acids found in natural protein (from living matter) contain only left-handed forms. Pasteur discovered this in 1844 by placing plane-polarized light through various solutions. Today, one hundred thirty years later, no one knows why this difference exists between the chemistry of dead and living nature. In all respects chemically and physically (except for the asymmetry) left-handed and right-handed forms are not only equivalent, but indistinguishable.

Coppedge[34] found that the probability of a living cell, composed of two hundred thirty-nine protein molecules (this is theoretically the smallest living cell possible) with each protein having four hundred forty-five amino acids, would all be left-handed (based on a half preference for left-handed amino acids) is one chance out of 10^{29345}. It would take approximately a half-hour to say the number in billions — speaking rapidly all the while! For comparison, the number 10^{28} represents the diameter of the known universe in inches! Furthermore, by making all sorts of generous concessions favorable to evolution, Dr. Coppedge computed that a single protein molecule would not be expected to happen by chance more often than once every 10^{262} years on the average. For the smallest possible living cell (two hundred thirty-nine protein molecules) it would take 10^{119841} years on the average to produce just one. If you assume the evolutionary age is $6 + 10^9$ years, then the odds against forming this one living entity during the entire age of the Earth is 10^{119831} to one! 10^{119831} is one followed by 119,831 zeros, enough to fill sixty pages of a medium-sized book.

Now this is only one simple protein molecule. When one considers more complex molecules like DNA which may be one million or more times as large, you begin to sense the enormous gigantic, titanic, stupendous faith required by those who believe that all of the wonderful, highly complex life in the plants, animals, insects, and humans came about by the same random process, billions and billions of times, over and over! Evolution is not science but physical and mathematical nonsense! This type of analysis prompted physicist Howard B. Holroyd to write:

> *"Physical scientists, who know higher mathematics and are capable of analytical thinking, should never have allowed the thoroughly mistaken mechanical theory of evolution to reach such a degree of apparent certainty in the thoughts of nearly everyone."* [55]

Similarly, Dr. A. Cressy Morrison (formerly president of the New York Academy of Sciences) wrote in the December 1946 issue of *Reader's Digest*:

> *". . . There is not one chance in billions that life on our planet is an accident."*

Chapter Four

Evolution And
The Second Law Of
Thermodynamics

But how does the probability of forming life by chance relate to the Second Law of Thermodynamics? This relation exists by the relationship between information theory and statistical mechanics. In 1948 Shannon[56] established a new field of mathematics known as *Information Theory*. Information theory is the quantitative study of information: its measurements and its transmission. Shannon defined information (I) as the difference between two entropies or uncertainties: one that (in reference to a question [Q]) is associated with knowledge (X) before a message and the other that is associated with knowledge (X′) after a message; in symbols,

$$I = S(Q/X) - S(Q/X') \qquad (1)$$

Thus, entropy is considered to be a measure of the degree to which information is lost or becomes garbled in the transmission process. In 1957 E.T. Jaynes[57] published a paper showing that by starting with Shannon's results, one could obtain in an elementary way all of the thermodynamic results of J. Willard Gibbs. The enormous conceptual difficulties inherent in Gibbs' approach were swept away. The text by Tribus[58] developed the relationship of information theory to thermodynamics for the undergraduate engineering and science students. The uncertainty or entropy of Shannon was defined as

$$S = K \sum p_i \, \ell n \, p_i \qquad (2)$$

where p_i is the probability of symbol i to the question Q and K is an arbitrary scale function. K is usually set equal to the ratio of $1/\ell n2$ (where $\ell n2$ represents the "natural" logarithm of 2). With this choice of K, S is said to be measured in bits of information. A common thermodynamic choice for K is kN, where N is the number of molecules in the system considered and k is Boltzman's constant, 1.38×10^{-23} joule per degree K. This important number is the smallest thermodynamic entropy change that can be associated with a measurement yielding one bit of information. One bit equals approximately 10^{-23} joule per degree K.

If one wished to mix half a molecular weight of each of two isotopes, the resulting entropy change would be $N_o k \ell n2$ where N_o (Avogardro's number, 6×10^{23}) is the number of molecules per molecular weight. Numerically this change is about six joules per degree K, or 6×10^{23} bits. This latter number represents the number of decisions that would have to be made if a person were to sort the isotopes one at a time. Hence, information can be thought of as the number of decisions required to "insert" a mixture.

Tribus[58] has pointed out that Shannon's equation,

Eq. 2 is identical in form to the expression used below in statistical mechanics for thermodynamic entropy

$$S = K \ln W \tag{3}$$

where W represents the "number of ways" a system can exist compatible with the restraints (thermodynamic probability).

In the more familiar classical thermodynamics, the Second Law is formulated in terms of energy. Lindsay[59] defines the Second Law in the classical sense as:

> *"It is in the transformation process that Nature appears to exact a penalty and this is where the second principle makes it appearance. For every naturally occurring transformation of energy is accompanied, somewhere, by a loss in the* availability *of energy for the future performance of work."*

In this case, entropy can be expressed mathematically in terms of the total irreversible flow of heat. It expresses quantitatively the amount of energy in an energy conversion process which becomes unavailable for further work. In order for work to be done, the available energy has to "flow" from a higher level to a lower level. When it reaches the lower level, the energy is still in existence, but no longer capable of doing work. Heat will naturally flow from a hot body to a cold body, but not from a cold body to a hot body.

The entropy law is seen to appear in three main forms, corresponding to classical thermodynamics, statistical thermodynamics, and information thermo-dynamics, respectively. Each of these corresponds to a different, although equivalent, concept of entropy.

In relating entropy to disorder, "W" in Eq. 3 is a quantitative measure of the atomistic disorder of the system in question. The Second Law of Thermodynamics was stated in the following way by Harold Blum.[60]

> *All real processes go with an increase of entropy. The entropy measures the randomness, or lack of orderliness of the system; the greater the randomness, the greater the entropy."*

Isaac Asimov[61] expresses this concept interestingly as follows:

> *"Another way of stating the Second Law then is: the universe is constantly getting more disorderly! Viewed that way, we can see the Second Law all about us. We have to work hard to straighten a room, but left to itself, it becomes a mess again very quickly and very easily. . . . How difficult to maintain houses, and machinery, and our own bodies in perfect working order; how easy to let them deteriorate. In fact, all we have to do is nothing, and everything deteriorates, collapses, breaks down, wears out, all by itself . . . and that is what the Second Law is all about."*

Obviously in our calculation of the chances of forming a protein molecule by random chance there was little hope of achieving this goal. The protein molecule represents a much higher state of order than the original batch of molecules. Entropy (disorder) tends to increase not decrease. The protein molecule represents a much higher degree of information (lower entropy) than the original batch. But isolated processes do not increase their amount of information or order, according to a general interpretation of the Second Law of Thermodynamics. Thus, there appears to be little hope for the evolutionist in developing a satisfactory scientific theory to fit the concept of evolutionary origins.

Some evolutionists will take refuge in the idea that, since the universe is almost infinitely large and we can only sample a small part of it, we don't really know that the entropy principle always applies. However, what we do know is that, wherever it has been tested, it always works. Even if a rare accidental spurt in some process violated entropy and created an evolutionary gain of some sort, the next spurt would undoubtedly be in the opposite direction and undo it.

Most knowledgeable evolutionists, however, if pushed for an answer to the entropy problem, will take refuge in the "open system" argument. Asimov[61] has stated:

"Life on earth has steadily grown more complex, more versatile, more elaborate, more orderly over the billions of years of the planet's existence. . . . How could that vast increase in order (and therefore the vast decrease in entropy) have taken place? The answer is it could not have taken place without a tremendous source

of energy constantly bathing the earth, for it is on that energy that life subsists. . . . In the billions of years that it took for the human brain to develop, the increase in entropy that took place in the sun was far greater: far, far greater than the decrease that is represented by the evolution required to develop the human brain."

In other words the Earth in its geologic time setting is "open" to the sun's energy, and it is this tremendous influx of energy which powers the evolutionary process and enables it to rise and overcome the entropy law which would otherwise inhibit it. The First and Second Laws of Thermodynamics apply only to *isolated systems* — systems into which no external energy can flow — and so supposedly do not apply to the Earth.

The evolutionist will also cite various examples of growth in open systems to illustrate his point — such as a seed growing up into a tree with many seeds. In like manner, he says, the sun supplies energy to the open Earth-system throughout geologic time to keep evolution going, even though perhaps at some long-distant time the greater Earth-sun system will finally die and evolution will stop.

This is an exceedingly naive argument and it indicates the desperate state of evolutionary theory that leads otherwise competent scientists to resort to it. It should be self-evident that the mere existence of an open system of some kind, with access to the sun's energy, does not of itself generate growth. The sun's energy may bathe the site of an automobile junkyard for a million years, but it will never cause the rusted, broken parts to grow together again into a functioning automobile. A beaker containing a fluid mixture of hydrochloric acid, water, salt, or any other combination of chemicals, may lie exposed to the sun for endless years, but the chemicals will never combine into a living bacterium or any other self-replicating organism. More likely, it would destroy any organisms which might accidently have been caught in it. Availability of energy (by the First Law of Thermo-dynamics) has in itself no inhibition for thwarting the basic decay principle (by the Second Law of Thermo-dynamics). *Quantity* of energy is not the question, but *quality*!

STEADY STATE
OPERATION OF
LIVING ORGANISMS

It is somewhat difficult to separate the relationship of the Second Law and the "creation" of life from the steady state operation of life. Of course, it is also recognized that in reality no such steady state operation exists (only "quasi-steady") since the organism is continually changing from birth until death.

How can we express in terms of thermodynamics the marvelous faculty by which a living organism delays the decay into thermodynamical equilibrium (death)? Schrodinger[62] stated it in this fashion:

"It feeds upon negative entropy, attracting, as it were, a stream of negative entropy upon itself, to compensate the entropy increase it produces

by living and thus to maintain itself on a stationary and fairly low entropy level.

"If W is a measure of disorder, its reciprocal, 1/W, can be regarded as a direct measure of order. Since the logarithm of 1/W is just minus the logarithm of W, we can write Boltzmann's equation thus:

$$-(entropy) = K \, \ell n \, (1/W).$$

"Hence, the awkward expression 'negative entropy' can be replaced by a better one: entropy, taken with the negative sign, is itself a measure of order. Thus, the device by which an organism maintains itself stationary at a fairly high level of orderliness (= fairly low level of entropy) really consists in continually sucking orderliness from its environment. This conclusion is less paradoxical than it appears at first sight. Rather could it be blamed for triviality. Indeed, in the case of higher animals, we know the kind of orderliness they feed upon well enough, viz. the extremely well-ordered state of matter in more or less complicated organic compounds, which serve them as foodstuffs. After utilizing it they return it in a very much degraded form — not entirely degraded, however, for plants can still make use of it. (These, of course, have their most powerful supply of 'negative entropy' in the sunlight.)"

Dr. Henry Morris[63] has listed the following four

requirements for a growth process:

"(1) An open system. *Obviously growth cannot occur in a closed system; the Second Law is in fact* defined *in terms of a closed system. However, this criterion is really redundant, because in the real world closed systems do not even exist! It is obvious that the Laws of Thermodynamics apply to open systems as well, since they have only been tested and proved on open systems!*

"(2) Available energy. *This criterion is also actually redundant, since the energy of the sun is always available, whether directly or indirectly, to all systems of any kind on the entire earth. As the Scripture says, 'There is* nothing *hid from the heat thereof' (Ps. 19:6).*

"Now, however, we come to the real heart of the problem. The evolutionist glibly gives entropy the brush-off because the earth is an open system bathed in the sun's energy. Such an answer is vacuous and trivial, since all systems are open to the sun's energy, but only a few exhibit a growth process, and even those only temporarily. What must be the remarkable additional conditions that can empower a worldwide evolutionary growth process in the whole biosphere for three billion years?

"For even the local, temporary growth systems with which men have observational acquaintance (as distinct from philosophical predilection), there must be at least two addi-

tional criteria satisfied.

"(3) A coded plan. *There must always, without known exception, exist a pre-planned program, or pattern, or template, or code, if growth is to take place. Disorder will never randomly become order. Something must sift and sort and direct the environmental energy before it can 'know' how to organize the unorganized components. The fact that a 'need' exists for growth to take place is of little moment to bobbing particles.*

"In the case of the plant, for example, the necessary program for its growth has been written into the genetic code, *the amazing system of the DNA-RNA complex which somehow, by its intricately-coiled template structure and 'messenger' functions, directs the assimilation of the environmental chemicals into a resulting plant structure like that of its predecessor plants. A similar coding system is also present in the animal seed.*

"In inorganic systems, the growth is directed by the intricate molecular structure of the crystal compound and by the chemical properties of the elements comprising it. Each crystal is directed into a predictable geometric pattern on the basis of the chemical code implicit in the periodic table of the elements and their own pre-existing structures.

"Artificial processes also have their 'codes.' The building is based on a blueprint and the dress on a pattern.

"But whence came these codes? How did the chemical elements acquire their orderly properties? What primeval DNA molecule had no previous DNA molecule to go by?

"Our experience with artificial processes indicates that a code for growth requires an intelligent planner. An architect had to draw the blueprint and a dress designer prepared the pattern. Could mindless, darting particles plan the systematic structure of the elements that they were to form? Even more unbelievably, could these elements later get together and program the genetic code, which could not only direct the formation of complex living systems of all kinds, but even enter into the replication process which would insure the continued production of new representatives of each kind? To imagine such marvels as this is to believe in magic — and magic without even a magician at that!

"A code always requires an intelligent coder. A program requires a programmer. To say that the most fantastically complex and effective code of all — the genetic code — somehow coded itself in the first place, is to abandon all pretense of science and reason in the study of the world as it is.

"But the genetic code is utter chaos in comparison with the complexity of a program which might conceivably direct the evolutionary growth process from particles to people over five billion years of earth history! Where is the

evidence for such a program? What structure does it have? How does it function, in order to direct elements into proteins and proteins into cells, cells into plants and invertebrates, fishes into birds, and monkeys into men?

"The sun's energy is there all right, and the earth is assuredly an open system, but by what marvelous automated directional system is this energy instructed how to transmute a school of jellyfish into a colony of beavers?

"Does the evolutionist imagine the mutation and natural selection could really perform the function of such an unimaginably complex program? Mutation is not a code, but only a random process which, like all random processes, generates disorder in its products. Natural selection is not a code, but only a sort of cybernetic device which snuffs out the disorderly effects of the mutation process. Is the evolutionist really so foolish as to think this kind of mindless interplay could produce the human brain — or, is it not simply that 'the god of this world hath blinded the minds of them who believe not' (2 Cor. 4:4).

"But there is still another criterion which must be satisfied, even for a local temporary growth process:

"(4) An energy-conversion mechanism. *It is naively simplistic merely to say: 'The sun's energy sustains the evolutionary process.' The question is: 'How does the sun's energy sustain the evolutionary process?' This type of reasoning*

*is inexcusable for scientists, because it confuses
the First Law of Thermodynamics with the
Second Law. There is no doubt that there is a
large enough* quantity *of energy (First Law) to
support evolution, but there is nothing in the
simple heat energy of the sun of sufficiently high*
quality *(Second Law) to produce the infinitely-
ordered products of the age-long process of
evolutionary growth.*

*"One could much more reasonably assume
that the sun's energy bathing the stockpiles of
bricks and lumber on a construction site will by
itself erect an apartment building, an infinitely
simpler structural project than organic evolution.
There is far more than enough energy reaching
the building site than is necessary to build the
building, so why bother to rent equipment and
hire workmen? This very reasonable suggestion
will not work, however, even if the sun's heat
bears down on those materials for a billion
years.*

*"The missing ingredient is an energy-conver-
sion mechanism! Some mechanism has to be on
hand to convert the sun's energy into the
mechanical energy required to erect the structure.
That is* always *true, for any growth process. the
natural tendency is to decay, so that for growth
to take place, some very special and effective
mechanism must be superimposed to convert
the simple heat energy into the complex growth
system.*

"In the case of the seed growing up into a

tree, for example, the mechanism is that of photosynthesis. This is a marvelous and intricate mechanism by which the sun's radiant energy is somehow transformed into the growing plant tissue. Photosynthesis is so complex and wonderful a mechanism that scientists even yet do not fully comprehend it[64] involving as it does an involved combination of electrochemical reactions, bacterial agencies, and other factors.

"Similarly, various metabolic mechanisms convert the chemical energy stored in the plant into mechanical and other forms of energy which the animal that eats the plant needs in his activities. The plant's energy may also eventually be converted into coal, the burning of which may drive a boiler which produces steam for a generator to make electrical energy. The latter is available at the construction site for conversion into the mechanical energy necessary for the construction equipment as it is operated to build the building.

"Always, therefore, one or more energy conversion mechanisms must be available for utilization of the sun's energy whenever there is any kind of growth process. This is in addition to the pre-programmed plan for directing the growth process, which must also be available.

"But the most extensive and energy-demanding growth process of all — namely, the organic evolution of the entire biosphere — has no such mechanism! Neither does it have, as we have seen, a program. How, then, can it

possibly work?"

Concerning the requirement for a code, Dr. Bolton Davidheiser (who at one time taught evolution in his John Hopkins University biology courses, but later became an ardent creationist) has stated:

"In the development of an egg, there is increasing complexity. The entropy requirements are satisfied, BUT a genetic code is required. Without the genetic code the egg would not develop regardless of energy or entropy. The question is, what was the source of the genetic code?.

"In cases like birds building intricate nests of the type characteristic of their species, they use energy and entropy increases. BUT without the instinct they could not do it, regardless of their physical fitness and sufficiency of energy.

"Human beings can accomplish great feats of building structures, and there is no problem with the Second Law of Thermodynamics. BUT intelligence is required. A bunch of morons could play with bricks, sand, etc. and expend more energy than the contractor's workmen, but they would not make a building. Something MORE than the satisfaction of energy requirements is needed.

"The evolutionists say (bluffing, I believe) that there is no problem about evolution in regard to the Second Law of Thermodynamics because the energy requirements are satisfied. This seems like saying there is no problem about

building a skyscraper if only there is available mechanical equipment, a source of fuel for the equipment, and enough healthy people selected at random. (The people do not have to know anything about building skyscrapers; the only requirements being that they are healthy and vigorous.)

"In the case of living things there is needed BESIDES a source of energy, one or more of the following: a genetic code, an instinct, intelligence."

The answer to the source of the code is obvious to the creationist: *"In the beginning God created . . ."* (Gen. 1:1).

Chapter Five

Evolution And
Young Age Of Earth

FOSSILS

If evolution were true, then the fossil record found in the Earth's crusts should show a slow shading in the fossil remains from the lowest one-cell forms at the bottom layers all the way up to a man at the top.

Charles Darwin[66] recognized this problem himself, when he wrote:

"Long before the reader has arrived at this part of my work, a crowd of difficulties will have occurred to him. Some of them are so serious that to this day I can hardly reflect on them without being in some degree staggered. . . . Why if species have descended from other species by fine graduations do we not see everywhere innumerable transitional forms? . . . Why then is not every geological formation and every stratum full of such intermediate links? Geology assuredly does not reveal any such finely-graduated organic chain and this perhaps, is the most obvious and serious

objection which can be urged against the theory. . . ."

One wonders why Darwin ever presented his theory if he was so staggered by the geological evidence against the theory.

The geological record has also revealed the surprising fact that life in its varied forms made its appearance suddenly in the Cambrian period. Professor John Koltz[67] wrote:

"In what is known as the Cambrian period there is literally a sudden outburst of living things of great variety. Very few of the groups which we know today were not in existence at the time of the Cambrian period. One of the problems of the Cambrian outburst is the sudden appearance of all these forms. All the animal phyla are represented already in the Cambrian period except two minor soft-bodied phyla (which may have been present without leaving fossil evidence) and the chordates. Even the chordates may have been present, since an object which looks like a fish scale has been discovered in Cambrian rock."

World-renowned paleontologist George Gaylord Simpson[68] has stated:

"Fossils are abundant only from the Cambrian onward. . . . Darwin was aware of this problem, even more striking in his day than in ours, when

it is still striking enough. . . . The case at present
must remain inexplicable; and may be truly
urged as a valid argument against the views here
entertained."

Simpson later wrote:

"Fossils would provide the only direct evidence
in the earliest living things, but none have been
found, and it is improbable that any exist in any
form still recognizable. . . ."

Paleontologist Simpson wrote in 1965 that some new
work in molecular biology may be fruitful in "proving"
evolution.[69] However, many biologists who believe in
evolution cite students to the field of paleontology for
"proof" of their theory (i.e., see p. 414 of reference 69). It
seems strange indeed that evolutionary scientists in that
field point the student back to the first field!

Dr. Duane T. Gish has examined in detail the
relation of the fossil record to evolution in his book,
Evolution, The Fossils Say No.[70] Gish found not one
bona fide fossil that indicated a transition between
invertebrates, fish and reptile, or reptile and bird. He
stated that there has never been a single fossil ever found
with part fin and part foot, or part feather and part scales.
He pointed out that birds, bats, and insects all fly, yet not
a single transitional fossil leading up to these species has
been found.

The hope of establishing a missing link between man
and ape was dealt a serious blow when anthropologist
Richard Leakey published evidence that Australopithe-

cines were long-armed, short-legged knuckle-walkers, similar to extinct African apes.[71] Up to this discovery, some anthropologists had supposed that man had descended through an ape-like ancestor Australopithecus who was allegedly two million years old and was thought to have walked upright. But Leakey's discovery of a large number of bones of Australopithecines showed he did not walk upright, but walked on his knuckles and in all probability he was just an extinct ape. Even more shattering to the "ape-to-man" scheme was Leakey's discovery in 1972.[72] He found bones near Lake Rudolph in Kenya, East Africa, which are similar to those of modern man but were dated much older than Australopithecus and Peking Man, our assumed near-man ancestor. And Gish[70] reported that in a lecture early in 1973 in San Diego, Richard Leakey stated his conviction that *these findings simply eliminate everything we have been taught about human origins, and he had nothing to offer in its place!*

The fossil gap appears to be a very serious crisis for the theory of evolution.

LACK OF MECHANISM FOR EVOLUTION

In a debate with creationists at a public high school in Marionette, Wisconsin on November 25, 1968, Mr. Walter Valentine, a genetics instructor at the University of Wisconsin extension center, claimed that we can prove change in plants and animals and since we can prove change we can also prove evolution.[73] However, he was only partly correct. There is change in plants and animals, but these observed variations have always been within well-defined limits within a kind or species. Changes from cats to dogs, or rabbits to rats, or from one major kind to another have never been observed. The two mechanisms for change are natural variations (which follow the Mendelian laws of heredity) and mutations.

Natural variation can produce all the varieties of modern-day horses from just one pair of horses. It is possible to obtain fifteen hundred varieties from a Hawthorne plant[74] by natural variation but no one has ever observed it changing into a rose. Because of built-in variation potential, breeding and hybrid programs in the plant and animal world are possible. In the 1800s, the sugar content of the sugar beet was increased by more than forty percent, yet since that time no further increase has been possible. Corn production was increased through five or six successive generations of hybrid corn, but since that time no significant increase has been obtained.

Mutations are the only observable things in the environment which affect the hereditary portion of the life cell. Radiation, mustard chemical, and perhaps LSD will change the DNA, or coding structures.[74] However, the change is always an injury. Sometimes a harmful mutation can be used to achieve a desired result (beautiful roses, for example), but the resulting organism is always weaker and unable to compete or survive, and if left to nature, will revert to its original form if it survives.[74]

Evolutionist Julian Huxley[75] argued that only one mutation out of one hundred may be considered good and this is all that is needed for evolution. However, biologist Dr. George Howe says the chances of producing present life on Earth by the mutation-natural selection hypothesis is about the same as trying to have a house constructed by a carpenter who nails ninety-nine percent of his nails in the wrong place at the wrong angle and reads the blueprint wrong ninety-nine percent of the time.[76]

In 1966 mathematicians and biologists met at the Wistar Institute in Philadelphia to discuss mathematical challenges to Neo-Darwinism Interpretation of Evolution. Dr. Murray Eden of the Massachusetts Institute of Technology (Inadequacies of Neo-Darwinism Evolution as a Scientific Theory)[22] and Dr. Marcel Schutzenberger ("Algorithms and the Neo-Darwinian Theory")[21] both presented similar papers which reported on digital computer experiments which modeled the mutation-natural selection process over time periods similar to that dealt with in evolution theories. They both reported that their computer studies showed that evolution is not possible (at least less than one chance out of 10^{1000} according to Schutzenberger).

Geneticist Richard Goldschmidt of the University of California at Berkeley vigorously rejected the Neo-Darwinian (mutation-natural selection) theory of evolution.[77] He maintained there was a limit to the amount of change that could be accomplished through a series of mutations and hence mutations are an inadequate mechanism for evolution. He proposed instead his "hopeful monster" mechanism. He proposed, for example, that one day a reptile laid an egg and a bird hatched from the egg! However, the Neo-Darwinists dispute this and believe as Gish[70] put it, *"that Goldschmidt is the one who laid the egg!"* Gish also noted that *"creationists agree with both the Neo-Darwinists and Goldschmidt — there is no evidence for either type of evolution!"* There appears to be no acceptable mechanism for explaining the process of evolution.

YOUNG EARTH

A considerable amount of recent evidence has been accumulated which points to an age of the Earth and solar system which is far less than the five billion years assumed by the evolutionists. Recently Dr. Henry Morris, Director of the Institute of Creation Research, San Diego, California, and the "Dean of Creation-Scientists" published a table of seventy-six processes which indicate the Earth is "young." [78] I have been able to add four more to this list of seventy-six for a total of eighty (see Table I on page 97). "Young" means any age that is less than five hundred million years. Of course, this is an extremely long time, but small when compared to the evolutionary age estimate of five to six billion years. The importance of this table is that there is an abundance of scientific indicators which imply the Earth is young — in fact, too young for life to have evolved.

The ages in Table I are based upon uniformitarian estimates. This means that due to a lack of historical data, those processes in operation today were assumed operating at the same rate during the past. Most likely many of these calculations are vastly in error because the rate processes may have been quite different in the past. For example, the influx of aluminum into the oceans via rivers yields an age of one hundred years, and this is obviously too young.

It would be instructive to discuss all of the young Earth estimates in Table I, but space is limited in this book, so only several will be examined.

HELIUM IN ATMOSPHERE

The amount of radioactive helium-4 in our atmosphere has been used by Cook[79] [80] to obtain an estimate of the age of the Earth. Helium-4 apparently enters our atmosphere from the solar wind and the radioactive decay of uranium rock. It has been estimated by Faul[81] that the rate of efflux of helium-4 into the atmosphere is about 3×10^{11} grams per year. Cook[79] has noted that the rate of loss of helium-4 from our atmosphere is less than 10^6 grams per year and hence is negligible compared to the amount entering the atmosphere of 3×10^{11} grams per year. Since the atmosphere contains about 3.5×10^{15} grams of helium-4 dividing by 3×10^{11} yields about ten thousand years for the Earth's age. The values of one thousand seven hundred fifty to one hundred seventy-five thousand, years shown in Table I allow for uncertainties in the efflux rate of helium-4.

METEORITIC DUST

Hans Patterson[82] has reported that approximately fourteen million tons of dust fall to the Earth's surface each year. This dust is from the disintegration of meteors as they burn up in the Earth's atmosphere. I have computed that at this same rate, the Earth would have accumulated a layer of dust two hundred sixty-five feet thick, extremely rich in nickel and iron, during five billion years. There is no apparent evidence of such a layer, which allows one to conclude the Earth is far less than five billion years old.

FLUX OF CHEMICAL ELEMENTS
RIVERS TO OCEANS

The rivers continually carry dissolved chemicals from the continents to the oceans. Cook[79] has noted that about 10^{10} to 10^{11} grams of uranium flows into the oceans each year. He reports the total uranium present in the ocean is about 10^{15} grams. Hence 10^{15} divided by 10^{11} or 10^{10} yields ten thousand to one hundred thousand years for the estimate of the Earth's age. Similar calculations have been performed on thirty-two other chemicals, and their range of age estimates are listed in Table I. This is obviously unrealistically low, but one might also suspect the largest number (two hundred sixty million years) is much too large. The median age for all thirty-three elements is approximately one hundred thousand years.

JUVENILE WATER

Whitcomb and Morris[28] have noted that the estimates of the influx of virgin or juvenile water to the oceans from volcanoes, etc. is in excess of one cubic mile. Since the ocean contains three hundred forty million cubic miles of water, this suggests the Earth is less than three hundred forty million years old.

EFFLUX OF IGNEOUS ROCKS

Morris[84] has pointed out that ten cubic kilometers seems to be a reasonable estimate for the amount of new igneous rocks which are formed each year by flow from the Earth's mantle. The total volume of the Earth is about

5×10^9 cubic kilometers. Hence volcanoes could have formed the entire volume of the Earth's crust in only five hundred million years.

DECAY OF EARTH'S MAGNETIC FIELD

Physicist Dr. Thomas Barnes[85] in a remarkable study has noted that the Earth's magnetic field has been decaying exponentially since it was first measured in 1835. His analysis shows that its half-life is about fourteen years. Based upon a half-life of fourteen hundred years, the Earth's magnetic field would have been equal to that of a magnetic star just ten thousand years ago. Dr. Barnes indicates that the only reasonable source for the Earth's magnetic field must be free circulating electrical currents in the Earth's iron core. He concluded that the heat generated by these currents flowing against an electrical resistance would have been too large for life to have existed on Earth more than ten thousand years ago; hence, life has been on Earth less than ten thousand years.

SOLAR SYSTEM DUST

Our space program has shown that the solar system contains much dust and gravel. Dr. Harold Slusher has pointed out that this fact means our solar system is young — probably less than one hundred thousand years old.[87] The reason for this estimate is based upon the fact that sunlight has pressure, which would tend to push the small dust particles out into space and cause a re-radiation braking effect on the larger particles, which would cause their orbits to continually shrink until they fell in the sun (Poynting-Robertson Effect).

POPULATION STATISTICS

It has been reported by Dr. Henry Morris[84] that the worldwide population growth rate is about two percent per year. He further showed that if we assume it was much less in the past — say one-half percent — then the present world population of approximately three and a half billion people could have been produced in four thousand years. However, if man has been on Earth for one million years and increasing at one-half percent per year, then there would be 10^{2100} on Earth. This is, of course, utterly impossible since it has been estimated there are less than 10^{56} molecules in the entire Earth. Population statistics suggest that man has been on the Earth far closer to four thousand years than to one million years.

TOP SOIL

The late Karl Mickey, writing in *Man And Soil*, stated that

". . . the soil which sustains life lies in a thin layer of an average depth of seven or eight inches over the face of the land; the Earth beneath is as dead and sterile as the moon. . . . That thin film is all that stands between man and extinction."

Of course, there are places where the top soil is much thicker (thirty feet deep in the tropics), but on the average it is only a few inches deep. Professor J.C. Taylor has stated that *"it took nature five thousand to twenty thousand years to make six inches of top soil."* [84] That corresponds to an average of roughly eight hundred to thirty-three hundred years per inch. This would suggest that the age of the present top soil is only about six to twenty-five thousand years. This would imply that life as we know it could only have existed in a continuous form back six to twenty-five thousand years ago.

MOON ROCKS

Various reports have stated that the moon rocks brought back to Earth by our Apollo astronauts have an age ranging from two billion years to eight billion years. However, Cook,[86] Heymann,[103] and Coppedge[34] have pointed out serious flaws in the dating method. A summary of the objections to moon rock dates in billions of years follows:

1. The primary chemical elements used to date the rocks would have been vaporized or boiled off. This is deduced from the "glaze" remaining on the rock surfaces and the fact that moon samples are depleted in all substances which boil below 1,300° C. Rubidium, the key element in the rubidium-strontium technique, boils at 688° C and potassium, the main element in the potassium-argon dating method vaporizes at 744° C. Since the bulk of these elements would have moved out of the rocks, the small traces remaining would result in very old dates when the potassium-argon or rubidium-strontium dating techniques were applied.

2. Professor Cook and scientists at Rice University's Department of Geology and Space Science are convinced the rare gases (used for radioactive dating) cannot be used for dating purposes because they came not from radiogenic sources on the moon but most likely originated in the solar wind.[86] This conclusion was reached when it was discovered that the rare gases on the moon solids were remarkably similar to ratios of the same gases in the solar wind (a constant stream of particles emanating from the sun). Furthermore, Heymann and the other scientists from Rice University wrote in *Science*, January 1970: *"We estimate the average 'hemispheral' exposure of a 250 (micrometer) fragment to solar wind of present-day intensity was (around) one thousand years. . . . However, a calculation based on ^{84}Kr gives (around) ten thousand years. . . ."*

3. There is not enough helium-4 on the moon for it to be four billion years old according to Nobel Prize medalist Cook.[86] It is the same dilemma that arises on Earth. Cook's estimate of the upper bound of the moon's age is in the tens of thousands of years rather than billions.

OIL AND GAS DEPOSITS

Nobel Prize medalist Dr. Melvin Cook has studied oil and gas well pressures and the permeabilities of the surrounding trap formation.[80] His studies have led him to conclude that oil and gas deposits have probably resulted from sudden deep burial of organic material a relatively short time ago — five thousand to at most one hundred thousand years. This is directly contradictory to the evolutionary-uniformitarian theory that these trap formations have existed for hundreds of millions of years in some cases.

Cook points out that abnormally high pressures (up to eight thousand psi) found relatively frequently in deep oil wells suggests that the oil was not in the ground for a long period. Using the measured values of the permeability of the rock surrounding the oil well, it is possible to compute the time it will take for the oil to seep through the rocks to the surface and the infinity of the surrounding strata. Cook reported the time required for a typical oil well to dissipate in this manner are on the order of thousands of years, certainly less than one hundred thousand years. These calculations are based upon the fluid dynamics of fluid flow through porous media, an area of science that is considered to be well-proven and non-controversial.

Blick[104] made similar calculations for deep gas geo-pressured reservoirs and found that the high gas pressures could not last at ten to twenty thousand years.

It is interesting to note that in eight cases studied by Hubbert and Rubey[88] all the wells except one showed active seepage at the surface. This led Cook to comment:

> *"These facts are irreconcilable with a uniformitarianistic model, and even with a catastrophic one in which the sudden deep burial is assumed to have occurred millions of years ago, particularly in view of the seepage. . . . Apparently only the mechanism of sudden deep burial a few*

thousand years ago, not even sudden deep burial millions of years ago, can explain these results." [80]

STALACTITES AND STALAGMITES

Many readers have perhaps visited Mammoth Cave in Kentucky or Carlsbad Caverns in New Mexico and marveled at the beautiful stalactite and stalagmite formations. You may also have been told by the guide that these dripstone formations are perhaps hundreds of thousands of years old. Recent evidence has shown these age estimates to be grossly too large. For example, a "curtain" of stalactites has been discovered growing from the foundation ceiling beneath the Lincoln Memorial in Washington, D.C.[89] Some of the stalactites (composed of calcium carbonate) were found to be as long as five feet in length in 1968. The Lincoln Memorial was built in 1923. Hence, the stalactites grew at an average rate of one and one-third inches per year.

In 1971 stalactites two centimeters in length were discovered under a spillway ceiling of an old dam on the North Santiam River, fifty miles east of Salem, Oregon.[90] Evidence of vandalism on the ceiling suggests longer stalactite specimens may have been chiselled out. The dam was built in the late 1890s, but was abandoned in 1912.

An interesting article in the October 1953 issue of *National Geographic* revealed further evidence of the rapid growth of dripstones.[91] On page 442 is a picture of a bat cemented upside down in a stalagmite! Before bacterial decay and/or scavenger attack could take their toll on the carcass, it was entombed by calcium carbonate.

Based upon these three cases, it seems probable that the upper limit on the ages of dripstone formations in caves is of the order of tens of thousands of years.

SEDIMENTS

Evolutionary-uniformitarian geologists generally assume the ocean reached its present size and chemical condition about one billion years ago. However, geologist Stuart Nevins has recently shown that the amount of ocean sediments indicates the oceans are much less than one billion years old.[92] The ocean contains about eight hundred twenty million billion tons of sediments and this is being increased at the present rate of about twenty-seven and a half billion tons of sediment per year. Dividing the total mass by the present rate yields about thirty million years. There is sufficient worldwide evidence that rivers were bigger and had larger flow rates in the past than at present. If this is true, then less than thirty million years would be needed to produce the sediment. It is also interesting to note that at the rate of twenty-seven and a half billion tons per year, the present continents will erode to sea level in fourteen million years!

DECAY OF COMETS

Comets undergo continual disintegration from gravitational and radiative effects of the sun and planets as they travel around our solar system. They have been observed to diminish in size and break up. Some astronomers believe that the planets and comets were created at about the same period of time. If this is true, then if one can estimate the age of comets, then one has a measure of the age of planets.

Certain Russian astronomers believe that the maximum life of short-period comets is about twenty-five thousand years.[96] [87] However, Lyttleton[93] has estimated the maximum life of a short-period comet as only ten thousand years.

Concerning the age of the other type of comet — long-period comets, Lyttleton had more bad news for the evolutionists:

> *"In the whole age of this system, a comet with an average period of 100,000 years would make 4.5×10^4 returns to the sun, and if each one of these lost only $1/1000$ of its mass, through tail-formation and meteor stream production, the initial mass would have been more than 10^{19} times as great as the present mass — which at a minimum means several times the mass of the sun!"* [93]

One is left with the conclusion that the lifetime of comets points to a young age of the solar system.

CORAL REEFS

There is evidence that coral reefs, which appear to represent the accumulations of the calcium carbonate remains of marine organisms, could have been formed in a relatively short period of time.[82] Juenen, in his book *Marine Geology*[94] stated:

"Little has been discovered of the growth rate of reefs by direct measurement. Sluiter found that a new reef established in Krakatoa after the eruption of 1883 had grown to a thickness of 20 cm. in five years, or 4 cm. per year. Other investigators have estimated reef growth at 0.1 to 5 cm. per year."

This prompted Whitcomb and Morris to comment:

"This rate of growth could certainly account for most of the coral reef depths found around the world even during the few thousand years since the Deluge." [28]

ESCAPE OF HIGH VELOCITY STARS

Clusters are groups of stars much smaller than galaxies. The high velocity of the component stars are overcoming the self-gravitation of the cluster and causing the clusters to break up. Slusher has stated:

"The stars are diverging from a common point so fast that in some cases if their motion were projected backwards to this common point, the cluster could have originated only several thousand years ago. . . . We have many star clusters that are disintegrating so rapidly that their ages can in no way be on the order of a billion or billions of years." [87] [95]

This presents a strong argument for a relatively

young age of stars and hence of our solar system and Earth itself.

PROBLEMS WITH LONG-AGE METHODS

The two methods that have been used to yield long ages (billions of years) for the age of the Earth are:

1. Radiometric dating of rocks, and
2. Index fossils found in rocks.

The first method is sheer folly in that it utilizes observations made on rocks during the last several decades and attempts to extrapolate backward in time for billions of years. It is similar to observing the life of a seventy-year-old man for twenty seconds and attempting to describe his life for the previous seventy years. The second method (index fossils) is based upon circular reasoning. The assumed evolutionary progression of life is used to date fossils, which are then used to prove that life has evolved from simpler to more complex. The primary evidence for evolution is the assumption of evolution!

The most popular long-age radiometric dating methods are uranium-lead, potassium-argon, and rubidium-strontium. They are all based upon three assumptions:

1. The rocks were a closed system.
2. There were no "daughter" elements initially present.
3. Process rates were always the same in the past.

Not one of the above assumptions is reasonable, in

that they are neither provable nor testable. The concept of a rock system remaining closed for millions of years is absurd. For example, Henry Faul states in his book, *Ages Of Rocks, Planets, And Stars*:

> *"Uranium and lead both migrate (in shales) in geologic time, and detailed analyses have shown that useful ages cannot be obtained with them."*

Eighty percent of potassium in a small sample of an iron meteorite was removed by running distilled water over it for four and a half hours. This test caused geophysicist Harold Slusher [87] to state:

> *"This could move the 'ages' to tremendously high values. Groundwater and erosional water movements could produce this effect naturally."*

Concerning the assumption of "no daughter elements initially present" — this assumption is impossible to verify — obviously no one was present when such systems were first formed. Hence it is clearly possible that some of the "daughter" elements were created along with parent elements (i.e., some lead may have been created along with uranium). Clementson found very large amounts of daughter elements present in very young volcanic rocks.[97]

Radiometric decay rates are not deterministic constants — they are at best only statistical averages. There are some who believe that cosmic radiation and its production of neutrinos could increase the radioactive decay rates and hence throw all of these methods into serious doubt.[98] Robert Gentry wrote concerning his study of pleochroic halos:

". . . My investigations of the uranium and thorium halos disclosed a startling circumstance: the radioactive decay rates had probably changed considerably during geologic times." [99]

(Pleochroic halos are minute circular discolorations in sections of rock crystals and are produced by specks of radioactivity in the crystal.)

Scientists at Westinghouse Research Labs in Pittsburgh, Pennsylvania were able to lengthen the average half-life of iron-57 as much as three percent.[100] This is further evidence that radioactive decay rates could have been variable in the past.

Nobel Prize medalist Dr. Melvin Cook has pointed out that free neutron capture (lead-206 + neutron = lead-207 and lead-207 + neutron = lead-208) may completely invalidate the uranium method.[80] His analysis of uranium ore from Katanga and Canada showed no lead-204, little or no thorium-232, but a significant amount of lead-208. Since the lead-208 could not have come from common lead contamination nor from thorium decay, it must have come from lead-207 by neutron capture. This means that literally all of the radiogenic isotopes of lead found in uranium-thorium anywhere could have been accounted for by this process alone. If true, this completely invalidates the uranium-lead calculations of billions of years.

In the few cases where radiometric dating methods were actually used on rocks of known ages, they flunked the test miserably. The *Journal Of Geophysical Research*, July 15, 1968, contains a remarkable article which indicates that the potassium-argon method predicted ages from 0.16 billion to 2.96 billion years from lava (from Kaupuleho, Hualalai, Hawaii) which was known to be one hundred sixty-eight years old![101] Sidney P. Clementson, a British consulting engineer, recently made a detailed study of eighteen rock samples from twelve volcanoes as published in the U.S.S.R. and ten samples from Faial Azores, Tristan da Cuuha, and Mt. Vesuvius.[97] In all cases the calculated uranium-lead ages were millions and billions of years, but the rocks were known to be quite young! If calculated uranium ages are eons too large for rocks which are known to be young, why should they be assumed correct when applied to rocks of unknown ages?

In the last sentence of Clementson's article, he stated:

"This conclusion would fit the concept of a young Earth and a recent creation as deduced from the Bible." [97]

TABLE I

Uniformitarian Estimates — Age of the Earth

(Unless otherwise noted, based on standard assumptions of closed systems, constant rates, and no initial daughter components.)

Process	Indicated Age of Earth	Ref.
1. Efflux of helium-4 into the atmosphere	1,750-175,000 years	57-58
2. Influx of meteoritic dust from space	too small to calculate	59
3. Influx of radiocarbon to the Earth system	5,000-10,000 years	60-61
4. Development of total human population	less than 4,000 years	62
5-37. Influx of 33 different chemicals (uranium, sodium, nickel, etc.) to the oceans via noperlod rivers	100 years to 260 million (median value about 100,000 years)	62-64, 79
38. Leaching of sodium from continents	32,000,000 years	64
39. Leaching of chlorine from continents	1,000,000 years	64
40. Leaching of calcium from continents	12,000,000 years	64
41. Influx of sediment to the ocean via rivers	30,000,000 years	65
42. Erosion of sediment from continents	14,000,000 years	65
43. Decay of Earth's magnetic field	10,000 years	66
44. Efflux of oil from traps by fluid pressure	10,000-100,000 years	58
45. Formation of radiogenic lead by neutron capture	too small to measure	58
46. Formation of radiogenic strontium by neutron capture	too small to measure	58

97

47. Decay of natural remanent paleo-magnetism	100,000 years	58
48. Decay of C-14 in pre-Cambrian wood	4,000 years	58
49. Decay of uranium with initial lead	too small to measure	67
50. Decay of potassium with en-trapped argon	too small to measure	67
51. Influx of juvenile water to oceans	340,000,000 years	68
52. Influx of magma from mantle to form crust	500,000,000 years	68
53. Growth of active coral reefs	10,000 years	68
54. Growth of oldest living part of biosphere	5,000 years	68
55. Origin of human civilizations	5,000 years	68
56. Formation of river deltas	5,000 years	69
57. Submarine oil seepage into oceans	50,000,000 years	70
58. Decay of natural plutonium	80,000,000 years	71
59. Decay lines of galaxies	10,000,000 years	72
60. Expanding of interstellar gas	60,000,000 years	73
61. Formation of carbon-14 on meteorites	100,000 years	74
62. Decay of short-period comets	10,000 years	75
63. Decay of long-period comets	1,000,000 years	76
64. Influx of small particles to the sun	83,000 years	76
65. Maximum life of meteor showers	5,000,000 years	76
66. Accumulation of dust on the moon	200,000 years	76
67. Deceleration of Earth by tidal function	500,000,000 years	77
68. Cooling of Earth by heat efflux	24,000,000 years	77
69. Accumulation of calcareous ooze. on sea floor	5,000,000 years	78
70. Escape of high-velocity stars from globular clusters	much less than billion years	80
71. Rotation of spiral galaxies	200,000,000 years	99
72. Accumulation of peat in peat bogs	8,000 years	81
73. Accumulation of sediments for sedimentary rocks	20,000 years	81
74. Lithification of sediments to form sedimentary rocks	20,000 years	81
75. Instability of rings of Saturn	1,000,000 years	76
76. Escape of methane from Titan	20,000,00 years	76

Chapter Six

Evidence For Noah's Ark

Apart from the second coming of Jesus Christ, I believe that the one event which may occur in the future that will stir up Christians is the discovery of Noah's Ark. I have studied the evidence which seems to indicate it is still on Mount Ararat in Turkey, and I would like to discuss some of this evidence.

Mount Ararat is located in the northern part of Turkey, right across the border from Russia. The Araks River separates this part of Turkey from Russia. There are actually two peaks on this border — greater Ararat and lesser Ararat. From the top of these peaks, you can see far into Russia, and this area appears to contain the base from which they shot off *Sputnik* and some of their other satellites. It is, therefore, a sensitive security area for Russia. Mount Ararat is about seventeen thousand feet high, and covers about five hundred square miles. It is basically a treeless mountain. There are a few trees near the base, but none on the main part of the mountian.

There are permanent ice peaks year round. Basically, the ice and snow are found from about the fourteen thousand-foot elevation to the top of the mountain. At seventeen thousand feet, this makes Ararat a very tall mountain. In fact, it is taller than any mountain in the lower forty-eight United States. In North America, only

Mount McKinley in Alaska is higher. In fact, it may be among the tallest mountains in terms of the distance from the base to the peak. Of course, there are other mountains that are taller in respect to height above sea level. But in respect to the projection above the base, it is either first or second in the world. It is extremely rugged and a very difficult mountain to climb. It is thought to be of volcanic origin.

There has been a group of Christians living near the base of Mount Ararat for centuries; they are known as Armenians. Many of the Armenians will tell you that Noah's Ark is on Mount Ararat and that it is guarded by angels. One story they tell is that the early descendants of Noah would make periodic trips up Mount Ararat to visit the Ark, I suppose to have some sort of worship service there. They say that the evil descendants of Ham, one of Noah's sons, for some reason set out to destroy the Ark. They also say that God sent a mighty storm which buried the Ark in ice to protect it. The approximate location of the Ark has been handed down from father to son for generations. Also, according to their tradition, near the end of time, the Ark will be revealed to prove that the Bible and the flood are true. For years, we have had reports coming out of this part of Turkey that shepherds on the upper pastures of Ararat have occasionally reported the sighting of the prow (front) of the Ark extending out of the melting glacier.

When we look at the various tribes of people all around the world, we discover a very interesting fact. Almost all of these tribes have a tradition or folklore which deals with a flood, a family, and animals. In fact, when you examine these stories, be they Hebrew, Japanese,

Egyptian, Hawaiian, or Eskimo, they all are essentially repeating the story of Noah and the Ark. The fact that so many of these tribes and peoples relate this same story makes me believe there is truth behind it. When you stop and think about it, surely the descendants of Noah, as they spread around the world to repopulate it, would carry this story with them, and pass it on from generation to generation. As the population spread around our globe as we have it today, we would find that in almost every part of the world, the story would be there. That is exactly what we find.

In every continent, with the exception of Antarctica, we find that tribes of people essentially relate the story of the Ark to their children (see Fig. 7). The names may be changed somewhat and the stories garbled, and some details left out, but the story they are telling is basically that of Noah and the Ark. In fact, someone once did a statistical analysis of these many stories, and looked at various aspects of the biblical account and compared it with the folklore stories. For example, seventy percent of the stories said survival was due to a boat; eighty-eight percent said there was one favored family that was saved; sixty-six percent said the flood was due to the wickedness of man; ninety-five percent said the flood was universal; thirty-five percent told of a bird being sent out from the boat after the flood; and seven percent of these stories mention a rainbow. There's a saying in America that if there's smoke, there's fire. I believe that if there are this many tribes around the world telling essentially the same story, there must be some truth behind it.

In the past one hundred and fifty years, there have been quite a number of reports from different people who

FLOOD TRADITIONS

DR. JOHANNES RIEM···" AMONG ALL TRADITIONS, THERE IS NONE SO GENERAL, SO WIDESPREAD ON EARTH···"THE FACT OF THE DELUGE IS GRANTED BECAUSE AT THE BASIS OF ALL MYTHS, PARTICULARLY NATURE MYTHS, THERE IS REAL FACT···.

ASIA	AFRICA	EUROPE	N. AMER.	S. AMER.	PACIFIC
ANDAMANESE	BERGEMAL	DRUIDS	ALGONQUINS	ARAWAKS	BATAKS
ARMENIANS	CARTHAGIANS	GERMANS	ARAPAHOES	CAURAS	DYAKS
ASSYRIANS	EGYPTIANS	GREEKS	ATHABASCANS	INCAS	FIJIIANS
BABYLONIANS	HOTTENTOTS	GYPSIES	AZTECS	MAYPURES,	HAWAIINS
CHALDEANS	SUDANESE	ICELANDERS	CHEROKEES	MECHOACHENS	MELANESIANS
DRAVIDIANS		LAPLANDERS	CREES	TAMANACS	MENANKABANS
HEBREWS		LITHUANIANS	ESKIMOS		MICRONESIANS
INDO-ARYANS		NORSE	KLAMATHS		NEW HEBRIDESE
JAPANESE		ROMANS	KOLUSHES		SOUTH POLYN.
KURNALS		SLAVS	KWAKIUTLS		
MONGOLS		VOGULS	LENNI LANAPES		
PERSIANS		WELCH	MAYANS		
PHOENCIANS			MICHOACANS		
PHRYGIANS			PAPAGOS		
SYRIANS			PIMAS		
TARTARS			SNOQUALMIES		
TORADJAS			TEXPI		
			TLINGITS		
			TOLTECS		

FIGURE 7

state that they have seen the Ark high on Mount Ararat, somewhere in the fourteen thousand to sixteen thousand-foot range (see Fig. 8). Most of these reports have stated that the Ark was sighted in a region known as the Ahora Gorge. In the 1840s, there was a volcanic eruption in the Ahora Gorge region. Since most of the reports of sightings have come since the 1840s, there is speculation that this volcanic eruption perhaps removed enough of the snow and ice above the Ark that periodically a very warm summer that follows a very mild winter will melt enough snow and ice to make the Ark visible during August.

Let's look at what some people regard as a problem, which is carrying all of the animals on board the Ark (see Fig. 9). Many people have a hard time imagining a ship large enough to carry all of the different animals required to repopulate the Earth. A leading American taxonomist from Harvard University did a study of the different types of land and sea animals. He found that of the land animals, there are approximately thirty-five hundred mammals, eighty-six hundred birds, and about fifty-five hundred reptiles and amphibians, or a total of about seventeen thousand six hundred species. The sea animals we don't need to concern ourselves with because there would be no need to carry them on board the Ark. Was the Ark big enough to carry these seventeen thousand six hundred species of mammals, birds, and reptiles? If we put our pen and paper to this problem, we can show that the Ark *was* big enough.

The Bible tells us that the Ark was three hundred by fifty by thirty cubits (Gen. 6:15). Let's assume a cubit to be about twenty inches, as a cubit is generally considered to

POST – BIBLICAL REPORTS ON NOAH'S ARK.

1. JOSEPHUS – 70 AD
2. MARCO POLO – 1300 AD
3. ENGLISH ATHEISTS' – 1856
4. JAMES BRYCE – HAND TOOL TIMBER – 1876
5. TURKISH COMMISSIONS REPORT – 1883
6. PRINCE NOURI – 1887
7. OLD ARMENIAN EYE-WITNESS ACCOUNT – 1902 & 1904
8. TURKISH SOLDIERS – 1915
9. RUSSIAN AVIATOR & CZAR'S EXPEDITION – 1915-1916
10. CARVET WELLS – TIMBER – 1932
11. HARDWICKE KNIGHT – TIMBER – 1936
12. AERIAL SIGHTINGS – WORLD WAR II
13. RESHIT – KURDISH FARMER 1948
14. GEORGE GREENE'S HELICOPTER PHOTOS – 1953
15. FERNAND NAVARRA – TIMBER – 1955, 1969

FIGURE 8

WAS THE ARK BIG ENOUGH!

CAPACITY : 300 x 50 x 30 CUBITS = 2,083,000 CUBIC FT.
(if I cubit = 20 inches)

= 777 STANDARD STOCK RAILROAD CARS

ERNST MAYR (A LEADING AMERICAN TAXONOMIST) ESTIMATES THE
NO. OF LAND ANIMAL SPECIES TO BE :

MAMMALS	3,500	
BIRDS	8,600	
REPTILES	5,500	TOTAL = 17,600

NOW ASSUME ½ ARE CLEAN (7 EA. REQUIRED) 8 ½ UNCLEAN
(2 EA. REQUIRED) WE CALCULATE THAT THE TOTAL NO OF
ANIMALS WAS $[½(7) + ½(2)] \times [17600]$ = 79,200 ANIMALS

ASSUME THE AVG. SIZE OF THESE ANIMALS TO EQUAL A SHEEP.
A STANDARD 2-DECK STOCK CAR CAN CARRY 240 SHEEP.

THUS 79,200 ÷ 240 = 330 STOCK CARS COULD CARRY ANIMALS

THIS CORRESPONDS TO (330/777) × 100 = 43% OF ARK VOLUME

YES THE ARK COULD DO THE JOB !!

FIGURE 9

be anywhere from eighteen to twenty-four inches. Some say that a cubit was the distance from the hand to the elbow. A twenty-inch cubit would be somewhat conservative. The Ark was three hundred by fifty by thirty cubits, so that would give it a volume of about two million cubic feet. This is about the same capacity as about seven hundred seventy-seven railroad stock cars.

How many of these seventeen thousand six hundred species of animals were carried on board the Ark? We don't know for sure. The Bible says that seven each of clean animals were taken on the Ark. Of the unclean animals, only two each were required. As far as I know, no one has studied these seventeen thousand six hundred animals and determined what percentage of them are clean and what percentage are unclean. For the sake of making a rough calculation, let's assume that half are clean, and half are unclean. If we do this, it totals out to be about seventy-nine thousand animals.

How many animals can be packed in a certain volume? Let's assume that the average size of all these animals was equal to a sheep. That's probably more than large enough, because when you look at the various mammals, birds, and reptiles, you run out of large animals rather quickly. Sure, we've got elephants, rhinocerus, and so on, but there aren't too many of those, when you think of thirty-five hundred species of mammals. There are a lot of mammals that are very small. So, a sheep is probably more than adequate for an average size of all these mammals, birds, and reptiles. We know that an average two-deck railroad stock car can carry two hundred forty sheep. We know that the Ark is about seven hundred seventy-seven railroad stock cars in size. If we can get two hundred forty sheep in one stock car, how many stock cars would be required to carry a total of seventy-nine thousand animals? The answer is three hundred thirty stock cars. This is only about forty-three percent of the calculated Ark volume. It would seem that the Ark had adequate capacity for carrying all of these animals, with room left over for food and other items that needed to be stored on the Ark. Plus, additional space may have been necessary for animals which became extinct at some point after the flood.

As I mentioned, the size of Noah's Ark was something like three hundred cubits in length, which makes it about the size of a modern-day ocean liner. Of course, it would not need the engines, rudder, steering mechanism, or smokestacks or any of the other devices found on modern ocean lines. All it would have to do is float and remain upright and stable. Marine architects who have studied Noah's Ark and its dimensions tell us that those particular dimensions form a very stable ship. In fact, it's been known that many of the vessels made by the Dutch for sailing through their canals, have dimensions which are essentially scaled down versions of Noah's Ark. It is also reported that one of our battleships designed about a century ago, was designed by a marine architect who was a Christian. He reasoned that the relative dimensions of the Ark might well be used to build a naval battleship, and this was a very seaworthy craft.

Some people also wonder how Noah could build a ship that large. We don't know for sure, but it could be that Noah's sons helped in the construction of the Ark. He also had over one hundred years to build the Ark. I did some calculations, estimating the amount of cubic feet of wood that would be needed to build the Ark. My calculations show that if only fifteen cubic feet of wood per day could be laid, for six days a week, that it would take from sixty to sixty-five years to build the Ark. The time factor was certainly not impossible.

Another question some people have is concerning seeds (for the replenishment of the plant world). The Bible doesn't say anything about seeds being carried onto the Ark. Dr. George F. Howe, a Christian botanist, ran an experiment where he soaked the seeds of five different flowering plants in various mixtures of sea and fresh water. These were soaked for up to one hundred forty days. I'm not sure why he didn't run the experiment for one hundred fifty days, because the Bible says the water was on the Earth for one hundred fifty days after the flood. But he ran his test for one hundred forty days, which is sufficiently close to make his results seem worthwhile. He found that of these five different types of seeds he soaked in water, three of them subsequently germinated and grew after they were planted. So it is possible for some seeds to be soaked in water for nearly five months and still survive. There's also a possibility that God preserved these plants by having Noah carry on the Ark barrels of seeds, such as corn and wheat, partially for food, and later for planting. Some of the seeds could very well have survived the Flood by being imbedded in floating vegetable masses, trees, and these types of things, or perhaps floating around on animal carcasses.

When we look at the accounts of the past one hundred fifty years or so, we have some very interesting information. Some claim to have actually seen the Ark, and in some cases photographs and drawings were made.

These sightings have been across a broad spectrum — from English atheists in the 1950s on up to Americans in recent years.

RECENT EXPEDITIONS

There is an interesting story about a Frenchman, Fernand Navarra, who in 1955 and possibly in 1969 climbed Mount Ararat. Fernand tells a story in his book, *Noah's Ark, I Touched It*, that when he was a young man stationed in Palestine with the French army, his company went on a mountain climbing exercise. When his mountain climbing chore was over, he was talking with an Armenian friend who told him that since he was such a good mountain climber, he should climb Mount Ararat in Turkey and look for Noah's Ark. Fernand filed this information in the back of his mind.

After being discharged from the French army, Fernand became a rather successful businessman. He decided to investigate and see if Noah's Ark was really on Mount Ararat. His study convinced him that it was and he set out to discover it. As the story goes, on his third attempt, he discovered Noah's Ark in a deep crevice, and he chopped some wood off the Ark and took it back to France with him. He tells of how the wood was rather long, and he was afraid the Turkish soldiers might suspect he took it off the Ark and take it from him. So he cut the wood into small pieces that would fit into his nap sack and decided to tell the Turkish soldiers that it was firewood. In any event, he took the wood back to France with him. He states that the wood had obviously been cut or sawed by hand and covered with a pitch, or a tar. It was also very dense and heavy. He had portions of the wood carbon-14 tested in laboratories in Europe, and results of the testing indicated that the age of the wood was around four or five thousand years, which would date back to the time of Noah according to the Bible.

Apparently, Fernand Navarra and others who have sighted the Ark are very secretive about its location, because it is very difficult to get information concerning the exact location of the Ark. I guess it is a case of the explorer wanting to keep the spot a secret so he can go back and fully explore it. Of course, this is only conjecture on my part.

Several years ago I was giving a talk at Colorado State University in Fort Collins, Colorado, where I was asked to speak to a group of engineering educators concerning the correlation of the Bible and science. It's interesting that prior to giving this talk, I was out in the hall previewing my slides on the wall with my projector, when a gentleman looked over my shoulder and began talking about the slides. He had a very heavy foreign accent, and as I talked with him, I discovered he was a Russian engineering professor from a university in Moscow. I told him I was getting ready to present a talk on Noah's Ark and invited him to come in, but he had another meeting to go to. I asked him if there was the existence of a belief about Noah's Ark in Russia, and much to my surprise he said, "Yes, we know all about Noah's Ark on Mount Ararat." This really floored me and I asked, "Do you mean to tell me that in Russian schools they teach the existence of Noah's Ark on Mount Ararat?" He said, "Yes, they do." You can imagine my surprise, because as most people know, this type of material is not even taught in our own public schools. You can get this information in Sunday school classes, or perhaps a Christian school, but most public schools do not teach portions of the Bible. Maybe the Russian educational system is not quite as atheistic as we believe it is, at least not in this case.

In the latter ten or fifteen years, there have been quite a number of American explorers who have gone to Turkey to climb Mount Ararat in search of Noah's Ark. As a result, some rather bizarre incidents have been reported. There is one case where an American is reported to have crossed the border into Russia, and as I have said before, right at the foot of Mount Ararat is a river which separates Turkey from Russia. This American is reported to have crossed over into Russia and visited an old Greek Orthodox church, ran by Greek Orthodox monks. The story is that this ancient church contained some artifacts which were supposedly carried on board Noah's Ark, and the American managed to steal them. As I understand it, there is now a warrant out for his arrest in Turkey for climbing Mount Ararat without obtaining permission.

There have been reported sightings of Noah's Ark from the air by satellites which have been placed in orbit over the Earth. A friend of mine, Dr. John Morris, a former professor of petroleum and geological engineering at the University of Oklahoma, has conducted two or perhaps three expeditions to Mount Ararat. He reported to me that he had been contacted by a U.S. government employee, who told him of the existence of photographs in certain vaults in Washington, D.C. which were taken by one of our satellites. The photographs clearly show a ship in the ice on Mount Ararat. Professor Morris has been unable to secure these photographs from the U.S. government. Perhaps they are in the files of the CIA; we are not sure. He also related to me that a former photographer in the military flew over Mount Ararat for some type of mission and shot pictures of what looked like a ship in the ice from a U.S. military plane. The photographer said he took the pictures himself, but once they landed and the pictures were developed, they were classified and he was not able to see them again. So there are some interesting stories about the existence of a ship on Mount Ararat coming out of Washington, D.C. by some of our military people and civil servants.

Although the expeditions that Dr. Morris undertook over the last decade or so produced some hair-raising experiences for him, at that time he was unable to find the Ark. He related to me how difficult it is to climb Mount Ararat. There are a lot of very loose rocks. You might take one step forward and slide two steps back. If you sleep on the mountain at night, you can hear it rumble deep down inside because it is of volcanic origin and has erupted as recently as the 1840s; I believe it was 1843. Dr. Morris states that usually the mountain can only be climbed in August because that's the only month the weather is mild enough. Even then, the weather is not mild. There are high wind storms of terrific speed, and at night, the temperature drops many degrees below zero. Arctic type survival gear is required. In order to exist that high in the mountains among all the ice, snow, and storms, one must undergo mountain climbing training. Some of the more recent expeditions to Mount Ararat apparently were not adequately trained in arctic survival and mountain climbing, because they did not get very far up the mountain. John and his associates practiced on Mount Ranier in the state of Washington before they attempted to climb Mount Ararat.

Dr. Morris and his companions were struck by lightning once while they were up on the mountain. They felt that it was the healing hand of God that prevented them from dying. After being struck by lightning, John was paralyzed, and he tells how he was miraculously healed. He told another story that while he and his companions were climbing Mount Ararat, there appeared to them what looked like a Kurdish-type of man with a rifle. John's Kurdish was not very good, but he did recognize that the man was telling them that they should stop, turn around, and go back. John related to me that he and the other Americans had a prayer meeting, and they felt God didn't really want them to leave Mount Ararat, so they turned their backs on this man and started hiking back up the mountain. After a short while, they looked back and the man had vanished. Eryl Cummings has related to me that for some reason the Kurdish people are very superstitious about Mount Ararat. The Kurdish people are basically non-Christians who live in the area of Mount Ararat. Quite often they are hired as guides by people who are wanting to explore Mount Ararat. Many of these Kurdish people, however, will not go above the thirteen thousand or fourteen thousand-foot elevation, because they are afraid of something. We don't know what it is, but maybe it is the presence of God.

It is very difficult for people to get permission from the Turkish government to climb Mount Ararat. In many cases, expeditions thought they had all the necessary documents to climb the mountain, only to discover that when they arrived in Turkey, there was one more document and one more official who would not approve their expedition, although many had already approved it. Their expedition would be turned down, and they would be told to go back to America. Relations between the U.S. and Turkey in the last decade or two have not always been on a very smooth keel and sometimes it is difficult for Americans to get the approval they need to climb Mount Ararat.

About ten years ago, Dr. John Morris and his expedition found some very interesting artifacts on Mount Ararat. As I said before, they did not sight the Ark, but they did find a circular stone altar and near the base of the altar were rocks which appeared to have crosses carved into them. This makes me think about the verse in Genesis which tells about Noah building an altar after he had landed on Mount Ararat. Could this be that very altar? I don't know.

Dr. Morris also found many caves on Mount Ararat. One cave has two large stone figures carved in rock that appear to be guarding the cave. When you look at them, it is hard to tell what period of history they are from. They have on some type of headband or headdress, and they are holding two large rods out in front of them. It brings to mind somewhat the pictures of ancient Egyptians or Babylonians. This particular cave was sealed off. John said he went inside as far as he could, but he found more rocks which sealed the cave off. He related that if he ever goes back, he would like to climb down in and excavate this cave to see what is down at the bottom. Eryl Cummings reported to me that an Armenian once told him that when the Turkish Moslems were killing millions of the Armenian Christians back in 1913 and 1914, many Armenians gathered up their worldly goods (money, gold, silver, jewelry, etc.) and sealed them in a cave on Mount Ararat. This Armenian told Eryl Cummings that many other Armenians were angry at him because he was telling people of the existence of Noah's Ark on Mount Ararat, and they were afraid someone might discover the wealth of the Armenian people.

As you can see, there is a lot of mystery and intrigue surrounding Mount Ararat. If God allows man to fully discover Noah's Ark, and allows it to be shown to the public, it will be the greatest archaeological discovery of all time. In my opinion, and in the opinion of many others, it should make ten-inch headlines in every newspaper in the world if it is discovered. Many men like Dr. John Morris, Eryl Cummings, Fernand Navarra, and others, would like to be the person who uncovers Noah's Ark on Mount Ararat and is able to publicly prove its existence. I certainly believe it exists, and I hope you do too. I pray that God will allow us to uncover the Ark and show the unbelieving world this wonderful ship which is a forerunner of our Ark, Jesus Christ, who is the Son of God and the Savior of the world.

Conclusion

By this point, you undoubtedly have reached the conclusion that there is a very strong correlation between the Bible and modern science. Therefore, the Bible and science must be casually connected. The only adequate explanation for this connection must be God. Therefore, if you believe what God said in the Bible about science, then you surely must believe what God says about man's relation to Himself.

God says that all men are sinful. *"For all have sinned, and come short of the glory of God"* (Rom. 3:23). *"The heart is deceitful above all things, and desperately wicked: who can know it?"* (Jer. 17:9).

God says that all religions do not lead to Heaven; only those who come by the way of Christ can enter in. *"Neither is there salvation in any other: for there is none other name under heaven given among men, whereby we must be saved"* (Acts 4:12).

God says that trying to be a "good guy" will not justify a man for Heaven. *"For whosoever shall keep the whole law, and yet offend in one point, he is guilty of all"* (Jam. 2:10). *"Knowing that a man is not justified by the works of the law, but by the faith of Jesus Christ . . ."* (Gal. 2:16).

God says that you must put your faith in Jesus Christ in order to be "born again" and partake of the abundant life and enter Heaven. *"For God so loved the world, that*

117

he gave his only begotten Son, that whosoever believeth in him should not perish, but have everlasting life" (John 3:16). *". . . I am come that they might have life, and that they might have it more abundantly"* (John 10:10).

As an engineer who discovered the Christian faith as an adult in a Billy Graham Crusade, I can testify to the abundant nature of my new life in Jesus Christ. Even though I have failed Jesus many times, He has never forsaken me.

My chief sin before I became a Christian was my independent attitude from God. I felt that if a man had a college education and success there was no need for the crutch of religion. It turns out I was partially right: man doesn't need religion, but he does need Jesus Christ.

Perhaps you are in the same position I was in before I accepted Christ as my Savior. If so, you can know the reality of Jesus Christ in your life right now by bowing your head and saying this simple prayer of faith: "Lord Jesus, I know that I am a sinner and can never save myself. But I believe that You died on the cross in my place and shed Your blood for my sin and arose from the dead. I do now receive You as my Savior and Lord; trusting You and You alone for my salvation. Save me now according to the promise of Your Word." *". . . Him that cometh to me I will in no wise cast out"* (John 6:37).

References

1. Riem, Johannes, *Neve Christoterpe*, p. 193.
2. Rehwinkel, A.M., *The Flood*, Concordia Publishing House, pp. 12-13, 1951.
3. Patten, D.H., *The Biblical Flood And The Ice Epoch*, Pacific Meridian Publishing Co., Seattle, 1966.
4. Patten, D.H., "The Pre-Flood Greenhouse Effect," pp. 11-41, in *A Symposium On Creation II*, D.H. Patten, editor, Baker Book House, Grand Rapids, 1970.
5. Howorth, Sir Henry, *The Mammoth And The Flood*, Sampson, Low Marston, Searle & Risington, London, 1887.
6. Jaffe, Louis S., "The Biological Effects Of Ozone On Man And Animals," *Amer. Ind. Hygiene Association Journal*, May-June 1967, pp. 267-276.
7. Whitelaw, Robert L., "Time, Life, And History In The Light Of 15,000 Radiocarbon Dates," *Creation Research Society Quarterly*, June 1970.
8. Cook, Melvin A., "Carbon-14 And The Age Of The Atmosphere," *Creation Research Society Quarterly*, June 1970.
9. Cook, Melvin A., *Prehistory And Earth Models*, p. 16, Max Parrish Co., London, 1966.
10. Chittick, D.E., "Dating The Earth And Fossils," pp. 57-74 in *A Symposium On Creation II*, Baker Book House, Grand Rapids, 1970.
11. Jueneman, F., "Scientific Speculation," *Industrial Research*, p. 15, Sept. 1972.
12. Cook, Melvin A., "Where Is The Earth's Radiogenic Helium," *Nature*, Vol. 179, p. 213, Jan. 26, 1957.
13. Faul, H., "Nuclear Geology," John Wiley, New York, 1954.
14. Staden, A., *Science Is A Sacred Cow*, E.P. Dutton & Co., Inc., New York, 1950.
15. Morris, H.M., *The Twilight Of Evolution*, Baker Book House, Grand Rapids, 1963.

16. Clark, R.E.D., *Darwin: Before And After*, Moody Press, Chicago, 1966.
17. Morris, H.M., *Evolution And The Modern Christian*, Presbyterian And Reformed Publishing Co., Philadelphia, 1967.
18. *Handbook For Students — Evolution: Science Falsely So-Called*, International Christian Crusade, 205 Yonge St., Room 31, Toronto, 1, Ontario, Canada, 1970.
19. Koltz, J.W., *Genes, Genesis, And Evolution*, Concordia Publishing House, 1955.
20. Koltz, J.W., *Darwin, Evolution, And Creation*, edited by Paul Zimmerman, Concordia Publishing House, 1959.
21. Schutzenberger, M.P., "Algorithms And Neo-Darwinian Theory Of Evolution" in *Mathematical Challenge To The Neo-Darwinian Interpretation Of Evolution*, edited by P.S. Moorehead and M.M. Kaplan, Wistar Institute Press, Philadelphia, 1967.
22. Eden, M., "Inadequacies Of Neo-Darwinian Evolution As A Scientific Theory" (see Ref. 8 above).
23. Morris, H., *The Bible And Modern Science*, Moody Press, Chicago, 1968.
24. Collected Articles in *Bible-Science Newsletter* (Monthly), Box 1016, Caldwell, Idaho, September 1963-present.
25. Collected Articles in *Creation Research Society Quarterly*, 2717 Cranbrook Road, Ann Arbor, Michigan, 1963-present.
26. Davidheiser, B., *Evolution And Christian Faith*, Presbyterian And Reformed Publishing Co., Philadelphia, 1969.
27. Gish, D.T., *Evolution, The Fossils Say No*, Institute For Creation Research, Christian Heritage College, 2716 Madison Avenue, San Diego, California, 1972.
28. Morris, H.M. and J.C. Whitcomb, *The Genesis Flood*, Presbyterian and Reformed Publishing Co., 1961.
29. Gish, D.T., *Speculations And Experiments Related To Theories On The Origin Of Life: A Critique*, Institute For Creation Research, San Diego, 1972.
30. Burdick, C. and D. Chittick, editors, *The Creation Alternative*, Bible-Science Association, 1970.
31. *Biology: A Search For Order In Complexity*, edited by John N. Moore and Harold S. Slusher, Zondervan Publishing Co., Grand Rapids, 1970.

32. White, A.J., "Uniformitarianism, Probability, And Evolution," *Creation Research Society Quarterly,* Vol. 9, No. 1, June 1972, pp. 32-37.

33. Kuhn, T.S., *The Structure Of Scientific Revolutions,* Second Edition, The University Of Chicago Press, Chicago, 1970.

34. Coppedge, J.F., *Evolution: Possible Or Impossible?,* Zondervan Publishing House, Grand Rapids, 1973.

35. Standen, A., *Science Is A Sacred Cow,* pp. 60-70, E.P. Dutton & Co., Inc., New York, 1950.

36. Clark, R.E.D., *Darwin: Before And After,* pp. 15-16, Moody Press, Chicago, 1966.

37. Vance, B.B., and D.F. Miller, *Biology For You,* p. 580, Lippincott Co., 1950.

38. Savage, J.M., *Evolution,* Holt, Reinhardt, & Winston, New York, 1965.

39. Fairbairn, J.W., *Nature,* "Correspondence," p. 225, Vol. 241, Jan. 19, 1973.

40. Hayward, A.T.J., *Nature,* "Correspondence," p. 557, Vol. 240, Dec. 29, 1972.

41. Hearst, William Randolph, Jr., *The Herald Examiner,* "The Editor's Report," Los Angeles, p. A-4, Nov. 14, 1971.

42. Dyson, Freeman J., "Energy In The Universe," *Scientific American,* Vol. 224, p. 52, Sept. 1971.

43. Shannon, C.E., *Bell System Technical Journal,* Vol. 27, p. 379 and p. 623 (1948), reprinted: C.E. Shannon and W. Weaver, *The Mathematical Theory Of Communication,* University Of Illinois Press, Urbana, 1949.

44. Blum, H.F., *Time's Arrow And Evolution,* p. 14 and p. 119., Princeton University Press, 1962.

45. Prigogine, I., G. Nicholis, and A. Babloyantz, "Thermodynamics Of Evolution," *Physics Today,* Vol. 26, p. 23 and p. 38, 1972.

46. Hull, D.E., "Thermodynamics And Kinetics Of Spontaneous Generation," *Nature,* Vol. 186, p. 693, 1960.

47. Williams, E.L., "Resistance Of Living Organisms To The Second Law Of Thermodynamics Irreversible Processes, Open Systems, Creation, And Evolution," *Creation Research Society Quarterly,* Vol. 8, No. 2, pp. 117-126, 1971.

48. Davidson, C.F., "Geochemical Aspects Of Atmospheric Evolution," *Proc. Nat. Acad. Sci.,* Vol. 53, p. 1194, 1965.

49. Brinkman, R.T., *J. Geophysical Research,* Vol. 74, p. 5355, 1969.

50. Howe, George, "Origin Of Life," *Bible-Science Newsletter*, p. 3, Dec. 1970.
51. du Nouy, L., *Human Destiny,* Longmans, Green & Co., p. 34, 1947.
52. Coffin, H.G., "Creation: Accident And Design," *Review And Herald*, Washington, D.C., p. 393, 1969
53. du Nouy, L., *Human Destiny,* Longmans, Green & Co., p. 34, 1947.
54. Morowitz, H.J., *Energy Flow In Biology*, pp. 66-67, Academic Press, New York, 1968.
55. Holroyd, H.B., "Darwinism Is Physical And Mathematical Nonsense," *Creation Research Society Quarterly,* Vol. 9, No. 1, p. 13, June 1972.
56. Shannon, C.E., *Bell System Technical Journal*, Vol. 27, p. 379 and p. 623 (1948), reprinted: C.E. Shannon and W. Weaver, *The Mathematical Theory Of Communication,* University Of Illinois Press, Urbana, 1949.
57. Jaynes, E.T., *Physics Review*, Vol. 106, p. 620, 1957; *Physics Review*, Vol. 108, p. 171, 1957, *Probability Theory In Science And Engineering,* McGraw-Hill, New York, 1961.
58. Tribus, M., *Thermostatics And Thermodynamics*, D. Van Nostrand Co., Princeton, New Jersey, 1961.
59. Lindsay, R.B., "Entropy Consumption And Values In Physical Science," *American Scientist*, Vol. 47, Sept. 1959, p. 378.
60. Blum, H., "Perspectives In Evolution," *American Scientist*, Vol. 43, p. 595, Oct. 1955.
61. Asimov, Isaac, "In The Game Of Energy And Thermodynamics You Can't Even Break Even," *Smithsonian Institute Journal*, p. 6, June 1970.
62. Schrodinger, Erwin, "Heredity And The Quantum Theory," pp. 975-1000, *World Of Mathematics,* James I. Newman, Simon & Schuster, New York, 1956.
63. Morris, Henry, "Evolution Or Entropy," unpublished manuscript, 1973.
64. Levine, R.P., "The Mechanism Of Photosynthesis," *Scientific American*, Vol. 221, pp. 58-70, Dec. 1969.
65. Davidheiser, Bolton, private communication with author, June 1, 1973.
66. Darwin, C., *Origin Of Species*, p. 80 and p. 157, J.M. Dent & Sons, 1956.

67. Koltz, J.W., *Genes, Genesis, And Evolution*, p. 208, Concordia Publishing House, St. Louis, 1955.

68. Simpson, G., *The History Of Life In Evolution After Darwin*, pp. 143-144, University Of Chicago Press, Chicago, 1960.

69. *Biological Science: Molecules-Man — Biological Science Curriculum Study,* Blue Version, Houghton-Mifflin Co., Boston, 1968.

70. Gish, D.T., *Evolution, The Fossils Say No*, Institute For Creation Research Publishing Co., San Diego, 1973.

71. Leakey, R.E.F., "Further Evidence Of Lower Pleistocene Hominids From East Rudolf North Kenya," *Nature*, Vol. 231, p. 241, 1971.

72. Leakey, R.E.F., *National Geographic*, Vol. 143, p. 819, 1973.

73. *Creation Study Guides*, Vol. 1, No. 2., Bible-Science Association, 1973.

74. Ibid., Vol. 1, No. 1

75. Huxley, J., *Evolution In Action*, p. 45, Harper and Bros., 1953.

76. Howe, G.F., *Unpublished Notes*, 1972.

77. Goldschmidt, R.B., "Evolution As Viewed By One Geneticist," *American Scientist*, Vol. 40, pp. 84-98, 1952.

78. Morris, H.M., "The Young Earth," Institute For Creation Research Impact Series No. 17, *ICR Acts And Facts*, San Diego, Vol, 3, No. 8, Sept. 1974.

79. Cook, M.A., "Where Is The Earth's Radiogenic Helium," *Nature*, Vol. 179, p. 213, Jan. 26, 1957.

80. Cook, M.A., *Prehistory And Earth Models*, Max Parrish, London, 1966.

81. Faul, H., *Nuclear Geology*, John Wiley, New York, 1974.

82. Petterson, Hans, "Cosmic Spherules And Meteoritic Dust," *Scientific American*, Vol. 202, February 1960, p. 132.

83. Cook, M.A., "Carbon-14 And The Age Of The Atmosphere," *Creation Research Society Quarterly*, Vol. 7, No. 1, pp. 53-56, 1970.

84. Morris, Henry M. (Ed.), *Scientific Creationism For Public Schools*, Institute For Creation Research, San Diego, 1974.

85. Barnes, Thomas G., *Origin And Destiny Of The Earth's Magnetic Field*, Institute For Creation Research, San Diego, 1973.

86. Cook, M.A., "Rare Gas Absorption On Solids Of The Lunar Regolith," *Journal Of Colloid And Interface Science*, Vol. 38,

No. 1, Jan. 1972.

87. Slusher, Harold S., *Age Of The Earth From Some Astronomical Indicators*, unpublished manuscript

88. Hubbert, M.K., and W.W. Rubey, "Role Of Fluid Pressure In Mechanics Of Overthrusting Faulting," *Bull. Geol. Soc. Am.,* Vol. 70, pp. 115-206, 1959.

89. Whitcomb, J.C., *The World That Perished*, P. 114-115, Baker Book House, Grand Rapids, 1973.

90. Keithley, W.E., "Note On Stalactite Formation," *Creation Research Society Quarterly*, Vol. 8, No. 3, p. 188, 1971.

91. Sutherland, M., "Carlsbad Caverns In Color," p. 442, *National Geographic,* CIV:4, Oct. 1953.

92. Nevins, Stuart E., "Evolution: The Ocean Says No," ICR Impact Series No. 8, *ICR Acts And Facts*, Vol. 2, No. 8, Oct. 1973.

93. Lyttleton, R.A., *Mysteries Of The Solar System*, Clarendon Press, Oxford.

94. Juenen, P.H., *Marine Geology*, Wiley Press, New York, p. 421, 1950.

95. Slusher, H.S., "Clues Regarding The Age Of The Universe," ICR Impact Series No. 19, *ICR Acts And Facts*, Institute For Creation Research, Vol. 3, No. 10, Nov. 1975.

96. Faul, H., *Ages Of Rocks, Planets, And Stars,* McGraw-Hill Book Co., Inc., New York, p. 61, 1966.

97. Clementson, S.P., "A Critical Examination Of Radioactive Dating Of Rocks," *Creation Research Society Quarterly*, Vol. 7, No. 3, pp. 137-141, Dec. 1970.

98. Jueneman, F., "Scientific Speculation," *Industrial Research*, p. 15, Sept. 1972.

99. Gentry, R.V., "Cosmology And Earth's Invisible Realm," *Medical Opinion And Review*, Vol. 3, No. 10, pp. 64-79, Oct. 1967.

100. *Time*, p. 74, June 19, 1964.

101. Funkhouser, J.G. and J. Naughton, *Journal Of Geophysical Research*, Vol. 73, p. 4606, July 15, 1968.

102. Mickey, A., *Man And Soil*, International Harvester Co., 1945.

103. Heymann, D., "Inert Gases In Lunar Samples," *Science*, Vol. 167, pp. 555-558, Jan. 30, 1970

104. Blick, E.F., "Mathematical Modeling Of The Evidence For The Origin Of Deep-Earth Hydrocarbons," IASTED, Intl. Sypm. Applied Modeling And Simulation, Lugano, Switzerland, June 18-19, 1990.

About The Author

Professor, School of Petroleum & Geological Engineering, University of Oklahoma, Norman, Oklahoma
President, Blick Engineering, Norman, Oklahoma

Education

B.S., Aeronautical Engineering, University of Oklahoma, 1958

M.S., Aeronautical Engineering, University of Oklahoma, 1959

Ph.D., Engineering Sciences, University of Oklahoma, 1963

Professional Experience

Aerodynamicist on F4h and Project Mercury, McDonnel Aircraft Corporation, St. Louis, Missouri, 1958-59

Research Associate, University of Oklahoma, 1959-present

Instructor, School of Aerospace Engineering, University of Oklahoma, 1959-1963

Assistant Professor, School of Aerospace and Mechanical Engineering, University of Oklahoma, 1963-1965

Associate Professor, School of Aerospace and Mechanical Engineering, University of Oklahoma, 1965-1969

Assistant Dean of Graduate College, University of Oklahoma, 1966-1968

Associate Dean of Engineering College, University of

Oklahoma, 1968-1969

Professor, School of Aerospace and Mechanical Engineering, University of Oklahoma, 1969-1981

Adjunct Professor, School of Meteorology, 1973

Adjunct Professor, College of Medicine, 1974-present

Professor, School of Petroleum and Geological Engineering, 1981-present